To
Never Forget

A True WWII Story

by
Gys van Beek &
Howard Moebius

Co-written by Mariah Montoya

Table of Contents

Introduction

This is the story of a Dutch farmer, born and reared on a farm along the Rhine River in Holland near the German border. The little town's name was Angeren, where Gys van Beek went to school for the first two years. The next five years he went to school in the City of Arnhem, where he was forced to discontinue at age 13 to work regularly on the family farm. This was due to the worldwide depression.

He was drafted into the Dutch Army during the mobilization in December of 1939. During the German invasion in May 1940, he participated in defending the country in The Hague, while wounded. After the Germans bombed Rotterdam, when 29,000 people were killed in two hours, the Dutch capitulated. He was kept as a prisoner of war for six weeks in the Hague and then released to work on the family farm again…He refused several times to sign up for German labor. Instead, he joined organized resistance in October 1942.

This is the story of the bravest man I have ever met. A man of conviction. A man of persistence. He sees a goal. He knows what is right and then he sees that it comes about – that it happens. I was shot down near Angeren during WWII. Without question, without fear, Gys went right out into the field where I was hiding and picked me up before the Germans could find me. He did many other things that saved my life and I am eternally grateful.

Howard E. Moebius
1st Lt. U.S. Army Air Corps
Sarasota, Florida

Map of Holland

The Netherlands

The North Sea

The Hague

Rotterdam

Zwolle

Arnhem · Velp

Angeren

The Rhine

Germany

Belgium

Gys van Beek

Author's Note

When we immigrated to the nation of immigrants, America, we understood that to be accepted and to feel equal to the people around us we had to try harder and do better. We were made aware of this through word of mouth, stories told and retold, but little from written word.

Long ago, since the early development of the new American people, they had neither means nor motive to write or keep records. Few knew how! Life was tough enough as it was, but in the era of fast-moving cultural development, important connections with the past are lost or ignored. To counter this trend, we must write our experiences, both the good and the bad, in order to learn from the past. This will guide us for our future.

Life without history is life without roots, without meaning or purpose. History holds a vast reservoir of lessons for life and is a solid foundation to build upon. Just learning from the past could have prevented many mistakes – world disasters, countless casualties, immense suffering and grief. The best way to know where we're going is to know where we've been! Realizing this,

I started to write, encouraged by family and friends here and in Holland, in both languages. This story must be told to warn what can and did happen to our highest principles and ideals.

Remember, America, Justice for All!

Gys Jansen van Beek

The School of the Bible

I begin my story by mentioning an accident that occurred to me when I was about six or seven years old – one of my first memories. Not all of this thought comes from recollection, but from the many times it has been retold.

Some of the older neighbor kids and my older brother Wim had heard the "William Tell" legend in school. William Tell was a Swiss mountaineer whose reputation was widely known as a bow and arrow sharpshooter – and a patriot. When he was captured by the enemy, as the story went, he could obtain his freedom only by shooting an apple off his young son's head.

William Tell succeeded and regained his freedom.

The story spread throughout the neighboring countries and became a literal reality for me. I do not think I volunteered for the part, but I do remember feeling honored when the other boys placed an apple on my head and used a homemade bow and arrow to try shooting it off.

My mother found me unconscious and bleeding. The boys had scattered like rabbits. After this encounter, I was marked for life with a scar on my forehead, the shiny indent of an arrow that just barely missed the apple on my head, clearly visible now more than 75 years later.

****

Our farm's name was Brouwershof, meaning Brewery Garden. It was located in the middle of our village next to the old ruin of a castle called Roode Walde.

Huge, old buildings with thatch roofs were used to house cattle during the winter – but during the summers, they attracted my siblings and the neighbor kids. We played soccer on the farm, or spent long hours trekking along canals and ditches, trying to snare something with a wire loop fastened to the end of a willow stick. Sometimes, Mother would cook the salmon I caught in the Rhine River that flowed on the outskirts of Angeren.

I went to school in Angeren until second grade, when my parents made my three grade-school siblings and me go to a large school in Arnhem instead, because they disapproved of the village's teachers. The four of us would leave home early in the morning and walk thirty minutes to a tram. Then we'd take a half-hour ride on this small tram pulled by a steam-powered locomotive until we arrived at the city. "The School of the Bible" was painted in large, red letters on the school's front wall.

The attitude of the city kids toward us farm boys was unpleasant right from the start. "*Stinkende*!" they called after us. "*Vuile*!" One boy in particular teased me nonstop, because I sometimes smelled like my farm animals. But what else would I smell like when I had to milk the cows every morning?

After a few months, however, matters improved rapidly, especially since I became one of the best students. A girl named Annie van Maurik was also one of the smartest in the school. Many boys admired her, including me. She was a brilliant student. This experience taught me a valuable lesson early in life that no matter what, nothing draws respect more than performance and behavior. Later on, I often wondered what became of Annie and the others. We never had a class reunion after the war, nor did we have any contact with each other.

The School of the Bible stood next to the Rhine River. Facilities for loading and unloading river boats sat next to the playground, so riverboats often lay at anchor, loaded with grain and corn that was unloaded by tough-looking men. Hoisted on the men's backs, sacks of grain were carried out of the boat and across the street into a building, where they were stored in silos. All day long, these men preformed their grueling and dirty work, which I watched in disbelief during school breaks.

But perhaps more wondrous were the shippers' children. These kids attended our school when they were in town, but sometimes we did not see them for weeks, or even months at a time. All at once, they would be in front of me again with stories of where they had traveled. Sometimes while visiting other countries, they learned to speak fluent French or German. I became enthralled with the weird, foreign words coming from their mouths.

During winter, I often visited the ships and saw the living quarters. They were so small and clean compared to our housing on the farm. I admit now, that when it was cold at the farm, I often longed for the coziness of the ships and something warm to drink.

When I was ten, I purchased a second-hand bicycle for sixteen guilders. Some of this money I had saved up myself. In the morning, I often helped the caretaker of our school by carrying buckets of coal to each of the nine classroom stoves. The caretaker's name was Mr. Blokland. He was a small, middle-aged man who sometimes gave me a few coins for my help.

While in sixth grade during 1931, we received French, German, and English lessons. I still remember part of a poem about the Depression that I copied on the blackboard for all the students to see:

> Come, fellows, the world needs mending
> Let none sit down and rest
> But go to work like heroes and nobly do your best
> Do what you can for fellow men
> With honest heart and truth
> Much can be done by everyone,
> Rewards for all who do.

I remember this poem because I was honored for my good handwriting by writing a message for the school's 100th year of existence on all the blackboards in each room. I was very proud.

Bruises and a Bully

Everybody talked about the worldwide Depression during my seventh school year: how many people were out of work or how awful the living conditions were. My chance of staying in school grew slim. Sometimes I overheard my parents' whispered conversations concerning me quitting school and working on the farm. I knew one of our workmen would be let go, and I would have to take his place. I felt so sorry for this man. He had a family of five children to support on unbelievably low wages.

Still, my father kept me in school for as long as he could. Even when we could hardly afford food ourselves, he would sometimes send me on missions, usually in the dark of night, to ride my bike and deliver a side of ham or bacon to suffering families. He gave me strict orders to tell no one.

I continued school, although my enjoyment in learning diminished, mostly because one of the older students teased me during lunch time. Smaller boys took beatings and much abuse from this older boy – I think he received boxing lessons one way or another.

When the end of my schooling became inevitable, I planned to get back at him. Although I was not a fighting type of youngster, I consulted some of my friends about the plan. They all laughed and discouraged me, but when they realized I was serious, offered to help if I started it. They hated him, too.

Since I didn't like the idea of help, I waited for a chance to do it alone when the teachers were absent. Usually when fights occurred near the school, the teachers always separated the fighters. That was the rule.

One day, after the boy had let the air out of my bicycle tires again, I confronted him and was quickly punched in the nose. It was finally my chance. I fought back.

I remember the triumphant look in his eyes. He and most of the other boys did not think I stood a chance. However, I felt fairly good about this fight because I had wrestling experience and I knew a few tricks. I knew I had to stay away from his fists.

He beat me up so badly, but somehow I found the courage to keep going. My friends told me later how the fight went. Slowly, I gained. That was when the 6th grade teacher came on the scene. Mr. Fraasen saw me all bloodied, but did not interfere. Why, I never knew.

When I finally got my first enemy pinned to the ground, he received what was long overdue. The boys told me how Mr. Fraasen formed a ring around us right in front of the school building, letting us continue – against the rules.

I never saw the teacher during the fight or understood what he had done until afterward. When I finally stopped punching the boy beneath me, he sent me inside to get cleaned up. As I walked away, I could have sworn he gave me a nod and a smile.

I learned a lifelong lesson from that childhood fight: never give up if the cause is worth fighting for.

Work on the Farm

I helped on the home farm performing all kinds of work. When I was fourteen, my parents entrusted me to plow with three, big draft horses.

My oldest brother Wim also plowed with three horses. We would compete with each other to see who had the straightest furrows. My family also kept 15 to 20 milk cows that we milked by hand, but nobody could beat Wim at hand-milking.

I excelled in gymnastics and sports, especially pole-vaulting and rope-climbing. We also played soccer with the neighbor kids every chance we got. In the winter, during bad weather, we played inside the cow barns, using the light from kerosene lamps placed on the ground. We put down straw and organized wrestling matches, weight lifting competitions, and rope climbing. Or if we were too physically exhausted, we played checkers or cards using marbles as money. We always made our own fun.

I loved to read the books at our small library in town. I also purchased second-hand books in the city for a dime each. The Carl May books about Indians were my favorite. They were so fascinating, written about the great American West in the early pioneer days. I also read about Negro slave exploitation in the book *Uncle Tom's Cabin.*

Gradually, life seemed to improve, as the sound of laughter and singing was heard on the streets again. Germany's buildup allowed Holland to begin exporting goods once more. After dealing with German horse buyers, my father urged me to learn German fluently. He predicted that Germany would overrun and conquer Europe, although he always frowned when he said so. I specifically remember him asking the German horse buyers, once, what they thought about Hitler.

"I like him," one horse buyer said. "He comes up with good ideas."

"Yes," said the other, "like his ideas with the Jews."

At the warning look in my father's eyes, I knew to keep quiet.

When Wim was drafted into the Dutch Army in 1936, I worked full time on the farm to replace him. But during the winter in the evenings, I took private lessons in Arnhem. At least two or three evenings per week I learned English, German, and bookkeeping. I loved it. The teacher's name was

Kurt Peneder, a German living in Arnhem who taught the classes in a room in his own house.

Sometimes it was hard to break away from the cozy fireplace to ride the bicycle six miles to Arnhem. It was especially tempting to skip the lessons in bad weather. But no matter how late I came home, my mother always waited for me. Often, I returned soaking wet. Our, big stove in the living room was the only heat source for the entire house, but it was a cozy place to sit by after coming home, and Mother always had it on for me by the time I stomped through the door. She was a true example of greatness, but I never realized it until later, after the war.

Hunting Stories and Gypsies

While growing up on Brouwershof, I remember big hunting drives held during the fall. Gentlemen hunters would pull up in fancy, horse-drawn coaches with their dogs, ready to engage in mass killings. They alone, with all their money, were allowed to shoot game on the neighbors' and our farms. We and other selected townspeople had to drive out game for the hunters by beating the bushes with sticks.

Sometimes I hid because I detested this practice. Perhaps I listened too closely to stories from my mother's uncle, Gerard Rynberk, an American veterinarian who had retired in Holland.

"In America," he told me, "everybody has hunting rights, not just a privileged few."

This same uncle had married an American lady and raised a nice family as a vet. They were all musically talented. A large portrait of them hung in our front room, one I often looked at with admiration.

****

A prominent landmark for each year was the arrival of the Gypsies. A few days before they appeared, the local constable would warn my father to lock the barns and chicken coups, because the Gypsies always stopped and rested for a few days on farms like ours.

But my father always treated the Gypsies with respect. They had a century-old custom he liked to accommodate by putting out straw for the people and their livestock. We had a small pond for them to water their animals, and we filled milk cans with clean drinking water. My father also put out firewood for them, saying to us, "The milk cans never disappear, you know."

They came in groups of ten or so wagons, each pulled by light and spirited horses. Some had colts at their sides, jumping and skidding. When the Gypsies settled down, the ladies and men went different ways. The ladies, with their dark complexion and slender build, went into the fields to gather wild plants for medicinal purposes. Some of the older ones went into town to sell cloth and trinkets.

The men tried to sell artistic jewelry or surplus horses. A few, both ladies and men, went from house to house practicing hand-reading. Once, my father held out his big hands while the reader followed his lines with her tiny brown ones.

At night, the Gypsies sang and danced to guitar music around a campfire. They were agile, supple people, some performing acrobatic maneuvers. It was remarkable to watch! After these performances, they passed a hat around, collecting a few coins.

When the Germans occupied Holland in 1940, the Gypsies never visited our village again. They were classified as an unproductive and unworthy race. The Nazis called them *untermenschen* – lower people, or parasites. As the war progressed, Gypsies were rounded up like cattle. Once, I witnessed such a roundup of these brave people. The men fought like lions with knives and primitive weapons, choosing death over getting arrested.

It was horrible to watch, even from a distance.

Joining the Dutch Army

Late in 1939, when I was 20 years old, I was drafted into the Dutch Army and stationed near Leiden with a horse-drawn artillery regiment. Soon after, I was moved to an old compound. It was so bitter-cold there, and all the plumbing froze.

The ships by the School of the Bible, I would think with longing.

One morning, my name was called to be shipped out to a place I didn't know. I had been selected to go to Breda, a brand-new compound with central heating and running water for showers. It was an instructional school for enlisted men to become officers.

I don't know why I was transferred to this new facility. I did not have one single diploma, while most of the other young men had advanced education under their belts. It puzzled me, but I was happy to be among other young men who enjoyed learning.

One day, we participated in an endurance match. About 900 of us men started marching early in the morning with full packs on our backs and no food to eat. Almost all dropped out, and by evening, only eight arrived at the compound. I was one of them.

For a simple farm boy, all of this activity was so interesting, and I hungered to learn. But I objected to the purpose of it all. Training to become a killer was hard for me to comprehend.

My first exposure to the methods of modern warfare transpired me when I saw a book with colored illustrations produced by the German Army. A soldier named Joop Rozyn, who was pro-German, owned the book. When I read the instructions, I immediately realized that our training was child's play in comparison. The Germans already possessed the most modern motorized equipment possible: airplanes and U-boats – all unbelievable to me.

At the end of March 1940, just days before my 21st birthday, I was promoted to corporal and moved to The Hague for practical experience. While stationed in the old Frederiks compound, I stood watch at the Peace Palace, a palace built and paid for by an American named Andrew Carnegie. The Peace Palace was built in Holland because the Dutch had the truest and most advanced judicial system in the world at that time. It represented peace and justice to all nations.

The German Invasion

May 10, 1940 – we awakened to the sound of German planes swarming over The Hague. Bombs whistled to earth, erupting with thunderous explosions that shook the ground. Anti-aircraft guns were immediately fired back by the Dutch, creating a crescendo of destructive sounds.

Everyone was ordered to take shelter downstairs in the cellar. In the panic, many soldiers jumped from upper floors to the landing I was on, falling on top of me. When I buckled, hundreds of feet started trampling my back and legs.

I cried out, and finally, a few soldiers helped me up, saw how injured I was, and carried me downstairs to a first-aid center.

I had a dislocated arm and a back injury.

"You must be hospitalized," a fretful nurse said, scurrying this way and that while the continuing battle outside made the room boom and shake.

"Give me treatment," I said. "And a gun."

There was a war raging outside, and I wasn't just going to sit in a hospital.

So, though the nurse put my right hand in a sling, I was issued a pistol with five rounds and ordered to defend – out of all things – a bridge!

Four other men armed with rifles were ordered to do the same. When we heard the orders, we looked at each other with astonishment and surprise. The bridge was located near an airport serving The Hague. German paratroopers had supposedly dropped nearby before daylight.

"Soldiers," our sergeant told us. "You defend that bridge at all costs. Shoot with the intent to kill."

We watched the bridge day and night for the next three days, billeted in a nearby house with its older occupants. The old couple cared for us by providing food and drink, but while there, we had no connection with other units. The only news we received, which was not favorable, came from an old radio in the house.

On the fourth day of fighting, May 14, the big harbor city Rotterdam was bombed and approximately 19,000 innocent people died in two hours. This act was followed by the threat that Amsterdam would be bombed next if the Dutch would not capitulate. Then we heard news on the radio that the Queen had fled to England with all the ministers and important government people.

To nobody's surprise, our surrender was announced over the radio the following day. We were outmatched by brute strength and superior modern destructive power.

Taken Prisoner

My fellow armed men and I received orders to return to our *oude Frederiks* compound in The Hague. As we came into the compound through the large, steel entrance gates, we saw a Luftwaffe pilot, from the German air force branch, tied to a flag pole. Hands behind his back, he was just standing in the middle of the plaza, intently looking everyone straight in the eye.

It was chaos in the compound. During the four days we still attempted to fight, we received constant incoming gunfire, but could not determine from where or by whom. When the orders finally came to lay down our arms, many men went hysterical, wishing to keep fighting. Some had to be locked up.

The Germans took over The Hague, and about 3,000 men in the compound were made prisoners of war, including myself. I was miserable. It made me sick knowing that somewhere out there, my farm might already be undertaken by Germans combing the country, my family separated or hurt.

But a few weeks later, my name was called from the gate office. When I arrived there, my 18-

year-old brother Jan greeted me! My mother had sent him by train to find me.

I hugged my brother with all the pent up worry and frustration and fear that had been building within me, my throat tightening.

"The family?" I asked.

"Safe," Jan said. He hesitated, and I tensed. "One soldier from our village has been killed. Piet Kaak. But Mother and Father? And our sisters? They're alright. Mother and Father have been giving out free milk in secret. Long lines of people sneak to our doorstep each morning and we give out what we've milked from the cows. Kobus Romein – that neighbor kid – has been helping us dole it out."

"Good."

I received a pass to go with Jan thirty miles to Oegstgeest to see if Wim was still alive. To our utter delight, we found Wim a healthy prisoner in a large tulip-bulb barn. How happy we all were for the good fortune! Jan and I stayed overnight on the tulip farm, all three brothers alive and together thanks to our mother. If not for the stench from the burning of Rotterdam so far away, we might have forgotten where we were, and why.

"Rumors have spread that all military prisoners are going to be transported to Germany for slave labor," Wim whispered to us as we chewed on some fallen straw to appease hunger. "Some people around here want to escape the prisons and return home. Others want to go to England, follow the Queen."

"And some," Jan muttered darkly, "would be more than happy to join the Germans."

I looked at my two brothers, lost. "But what should *we* do?"

As if in response to our conversation, a few hours later, a Dutch captain in the barn climbed on top of a few boxes and gave a short speech to the assortment of pallid-faced men assembled at his feet.

"Never will we be a province of Germany!" the Dutch captain shouted. "We are and always will be our own people! Hear me now! *Don't* do anything foolish or unorganized without good and careful planning. Our government will continue to function in England and orders in due time will be given by radio. Be aware of the cruel and barbaric methods of our enemy and expect several years of war to bring him down."

At the words "cruel" and "barbaric," I was kindled with an inner fire I never knew I had. Wim grabbed my arm and asked, "Did you hear him, Gys? Don't do anything foolish without planning. We can fight back, though, if we're cautious! Did you hear?"

"Yes," I said. "I heard."

The next day, Jan returned to the farm with the good news of our safety, and I returned to the compound at The Hague like a good boy, so that the German soldiers wouldn't come after my family. I stayed in The Hague until mid-June in 1940, when all farmers were released to work at increasing food supply for the enemy.

I managed to stay hidden in my farm, keeping a low-profile for almost a year. When the German occupants and conquerors notified me to register in Arnhem to be a soldier for the German army, I simply didn't go. This was a risk. Many people who made that decision were caught and forced into slave labor camps in Germany.

Most of Western Europe was overrun, occupied by the Germans. Hitler and his cronies hatched a plan to jump on England after bombing the coastal cities, but after much deliberation and planning, they postponed this plan. To our surprise and astonishment, Hitler unleashed 120 of his best divisions into Russia on June 22, 1941 at the height of his glory days. Advancing deep into Russia, he employed brutal methods – but the feared Russian winter became his downfall.

I can remember my father saying, "After the killings of millions of innocent people, Adolf does not stand a chance at winning World War II. This will bring mighty *America* into the war."

On the 22nd of October, 1942, a local scout for the German Army, a man named Tut Vander Velde, marched to my farm's doorstep and offered me a position to become the leader of young farmers and make Nazis out of them. If I denied it, Jan and I would be sent to the slave labor camps in Germany.

To appease Tut in the moment, I let him interview me and take my picture. Then, when the time came for us to meet up again, I never showed up. Thankfully, Tut must have forgotten.

Jan was not so lucky. He was summoned to work in a German factory, but refused – a warrant came out for his arrest, so Wim and I helped him escape by hiding him in an abandoned farmhouse across the Rhine River. Because we didn't want to endanger him, we lost contact for several months.

His absence made us miss his humor and enthusiasm, but at least he was safe.

Realizing how close of a call that had been, I knew drastic measures of rebellion must be taken on my part. I would not continue to skirt around the Germans and risk the chance of getting arrested or shipped off unless I was doing something worthwhile.

This is when I joined the Resistance.

The Resistance

My looks helped me: blonde hair, blue eyes. It also didn't hurt that I was fluent in German. Coupled with this ability and false papers I obtained, I was able to act as a regular civilian, sometimes perceived as an Aryan myself while secretly doing undercover work as well. I resumed part-time studies with a Mr. Cees Smits, who was deeply involved in the Resistance and introduced me to all his work.

Sometimes, as I worked in the fields along the Rhine River, thousands of German troops stationed a few miles away in Arnhem made the very ground vibrate with marches and music. For most of us in Angeren, the sound of the Germans singing as they marched was blood-chilling. But the powerful music had tremendous impacts on the military forces – they were swept away by their imaginations and dreams of belonging to a superhuman race. This notion was transpired by the enormous propaganda and hysterical speeches made by Hitler.

The propaganda had a hypnotizing influence, especially on the youth. Even some of my friends,

Dutch people, who were good and well-respected, became National Socialistic Beweging members. They tried many times to persuade us, the four van Beek brothers, that they needed us for the fatherland.

Large posters hung everywhere and radio messages blared out, "WE NEED STALWERT, ALERT, AND GOOD-LOOKING ATHLETIC YOUTHS. WE NEED GERMANIC-NORDIC, BLUE-EYED, BLONDE YOUNGSTERS." Indeed, it was impressive and alluring for the innocent young Dutchmen to sign up. Sadly, many did.

Hitler figured out his tactics during his time in prison, when he wrote it down in his book, *Mein Kampf*:

> The products of human culture, the achievement in art, science, and technology with which we are blessed today are almost exclusively the creative product of the Aryan. That very fact enables us to draw the not so unfounded conclusion that they alone were founders of higher humanity.

Of course, this was not true, but statements like this had an enormous impact on recruiting. German unity could thus be maintained on the mere belief of pure and superior blood. It worked wonders in the early months of 1933 when Hitler came to power. Strict standards were applied by racial experts toward the selection of the first 50,000 super-men. Only young men who were perfect in build and movement could aspire to transfer to the feared SS. And of course, these young men were brainwashed into believing that if they made the cut, they were of a superior breeding and had the right to receive privileges others didn't.

The Germans marked one military victory after another in the West – Russia and North Africa. In the East, Nazi ferocity in the service of its negative population policy was exercised without restraint. Eleven million Jews and thirty million Slavs called "incorrigibles" were due for extermination by 1940.

Seventy million other "sub-humans" were moved to Siberia, Africa, or Latin America. The object of the positive population policy was to replace these "disinfected" populations with members of a master race. By breeding – or recovering, in Hitler's words – a hundred million Nordics, it would be possible to obtain the total of 250 million Aryans to start the 1,000-year Reich.

In Poland alone, more than 200 thousand children were kidnapped. The ten percent who passed inspection were utilized according to the German Army's plan. The other ninety percent was sterilized, sent to camps, or eliminated.

Somehow, I escaped the fanatic and devilish propaganda. I did not believe in the promises of rewards for being an SS officer, perhaps in part due to America finally rolling up its sleeves and plunging into the war against Germany, in December of 1941.

My father had been right. America's power began to make a difference. The highly-touted SS standards were lowered. Posters of young, beautiful soldiers in splendid uniforms were still displayed everywhere, but now death symbols could be seen drawn over their uniforms and caps.

The Allied planners selected Dwight D. Eisenhower as supreme commander to conquer the fanatics. This unique and most qualified commander selected General George S. Patton, a man devoted to the war, to lead the brave Americans into the world's fires. We all felt a wave of relief and hope for the future. It was a turning point. Germany's winning streak ended and their over-aggressive methods backfired.

American flying forces entered the war with daytime bombing. For some time, the English, Lancaster, and Halifax heavy bombers bombed Germany at night. But the Americans bombed during the day with their B-17 Flying Fortresses.

When the Americans came to Holland to bomb the Germans too, the Germans occupied the Deelen airfield in Arnhem with hundreds of fighter planes. German artillery pounded away at the American planes, bringing down many. From below, we saw eighty-eight shells explode. When a Fortress was hit, we anxiously waited for the crew to jump out with their parachutes to avoid the death of the crash. Often, they did not. Awful dogfights took place above our heads.

Every day, we listened to secret senders from the BBC talk about the great success of these Liberator bombers. No matter how busy we were, we always stopped to watch the breathtaking and horrible activities of the B-17's, and later the B-24's. When some pieces came hurtling down, burning close by, I raced on my bicycle to be the first one on the scene. If crew members were killed, I took one of two ID tags and kept them. After the war, I sent these tags to Intelligence.

We seldom helped daytime American flyers escape because they were too far away. If they were not already dead, many of these pilots were taken as prisoner. If they tried parachuting out of the plane from up high, it took too long for them to land; the Germans' specially-trained men were usually there ahead of us to pluck them from the air and take them captive.

Whenever we heard Germans coming, we quickly disappeared. Their motto, "Shoot first, then ask questions," was more and more practiced as the war shifted in favor of the Allies. The North Africa landing campaign had successfully occurred and the Sicily Invasion was also going in the Allies' favor.

For my Resistance activities, I hauled and delivered food stamps for the needy who were in hiding. Producing these food stamps and false ID cards was my main job. I always made sure to be careful when delivering these papers or stamps. Many who did as I did were caught by the SS and punished severely, or killed.

Once, when I was scheduled by Resistance leaders to participate in blowing up a railroad tunnel, I plainly refused, because it was risky and unnecessary. Later on, I was thankful I had declined this task when we were told that the enemy had discovered the plans and demanded for the culprits to come forward. When none did, many innocent victims were killed in replacement.

Marked for Elimination

Soon after the Germans occupied the Netherlands, the Jewish people became targets. Starting in 1940 these doomed individuals, part of the Dutch people, were marked as victims of the most barbaric, inhumane methods of elimination.

To start with, they were forced to wear a six-point, large, yellow star sewn onto the clothing worn on their chests. In the village, we didn't notice this much because few Jews lived in Angeren. But whenever I went to the city, I saw many wearing the Star of David, a sight which brought forth feelings of nothing but evil. Rumors circulated about a plan to completely eliminate the Jewish people. Few really believed such an idea could be solidified, including myself; we all thought they were only being hauled off to labor camps. But this didn't change the fact that Jews were being forced to register left and right. In the newspapers and on posters everywhere, they were ordered to report their names and addresses. Soon after, the first razzias – or manhunts – began.

These hunts were carried out by trained soldiers led by the SS and Gestapo men. They always appeared at unexpected times, helmeted, with automatic weapons, in trucks and on motorcycles. As the victims were rounded up, some were not even allowed to take valuables or clothing. I witnessed them literally being torn out of their homes, accompanied by the loud cries of "*schnell, schweinhunde!*" Fast, pig dogs! The people were then marched or hauled off in enclosed trucks. The victims were taken to and guarded in empty buildings until further orders.

Watching this was a terrible emotional shock for everyone. When these wagons and helmeted troops were seen in the city, people frantically spread the news. It was like a wave of terror spreading throughout the city. Systematically, that doomed part of the population was imprisoned. The Jews' businesses were plundered and boarded up.

Naturally, some fled into hiding, but I was always surprised why more did not try to escape. Perhaps through false propaganda, which seemed to be the German's specialty, the majority was misled – and loaded into cattle cars because of it.

It certainly was a blow to witness such a deprivation of people's freedom. I myself already felt half-enslaved, and observing these roundups of thousands of people was not only inhumane, but truly scary. Everyone became scared that if such things could happen to the Jewish people, it certainly could happen to anyone else.

The whole nation of Holland went on strike, but sadly, not for long. A score of prominent people were immediately arrested by SS officers and executed publicly. That is how the Germans operated, their methods yielding no mercy and knowing no bounds.

These heart-rending scenes of violence I saw in Arnhem, the families being harshly torn apart, only added to the kindling of fire within my heart. I had a desperate desire to do more, rebel more, resist more. I abhorred anything unjust, especially wrongs inflicted upon others with malice and intent to cause hurt or suffering.

I was regretful, and still am, that I was not able to help as a whole. Only once during those critical days, in a small way, was I able to give direct help to the Jews.

One winter day in 1942, I bicycled to the city train station. Coming near, I saw a small boy, about nine or ten years old, running away from a crowd waiting to be loaded on cattle cars. He had slid flat on his belly and squirmed under the train cars. Wild-eyed and in a great panic, he ran in my direction. German soldiers yelled for him to stop.

I made a ferocious gesture for him to hop on the back of my bike. The boy did and off we went, full speed, away from the station, the boy clutching my shoulders. A few city blocks later, the little fugitive jumped off and disappeared between homes. All this took place within a matter of seconds.

I never saw him again.

Seven Dead Pilots

During the early summer of 1943, we witnessed a burning B-17 fly over our village. It flew low and slow in its return from a bombing raid. These damaged planes were called cripples. I watched hopefully from below, praying for the crew to bail out. But none did. All at once, the plane exploded right above town, producing terrifying and deafening sounds. Some people stood in complete fear, screaming as if glued to the earth. Others ran for cover, afraid of burning pieces that might hurtle to the ground. But most pieces of the aircraft dropped outside of our small town between the Rhine River and the dike.

I was one of the first to arrive on the scene. I left my bicycle and walked toward the wreckage, which was strewn about in a pasture. Some of the larger and lighter pieces continued falling from the sky. I spotted a crewmember lying nearby, and hurried to him. As I was walking, I passed a hand, severed at the wrist, lying in the grass. I stared at it in amazement, with the screams of civilians still echoing from far away. Then I shook my head, continuing toward the body lying on the ground.

It was the tail-gunner – a small boy about 18 years old. He still clutched his machine gun, and at first, I thought he was simply sleeping, or in shock.

"Hello?" I asked, bending down to the boy. "American, can you hear me?"

The boy didn't answer. The only response was ash falling from the sky and landing on his stiff nose. Feeling dizzy, I realized he wasn't asleep. I managed to force myself on in search of any survivors. I came upon the burning nose section, where three officers inside their cockpit were still holding onto the controls, each coal-black and burned. I stared at them in a daze. I kept searching. I found three more bodies nearby, just as black, just as gone. They were the first Americans I had ever seen up close – all dead.

Sitting on the heels of my feet, I put my face in my hands and cried.

Before long, I heard loud voices The Germans had arrived, as usual – loud and aggressive. They parked vehicles close to my bicycle. I disappeared as fast as I could, disobeying their abrupt orders for me to stop. I heard some shots as I ran, but I do not believe the firing was aimed at me. Perhaps it was meant to scare people away from the scene.

I waited for the Germans to leave before retrieving my bicycle. I buried the seven ID tags and dug them up again after the war. One mother of one of the victims wrote to me years later. She wanted to know all about her son's death, and sent me a picture of him to me. He was the first victim I had found, the young boy. His name was Robert Walker from Waukesha, Wisconsin. I do not remember how his mother, Marie, learned of my address, but I still have some of her letters.

The Sergeant from Kansas

By the end of the war, ten more planes crashed in and around Angeren. On one occasion, we were finally able to help a B-17 crewman.

While harvesting cherries on June 22, 1943, hundreds of B-17's flew high above after returning from a bombing raid. One of the planes was on fire. One by one, all ten of the crew jumped out, their parachutes like small snowballs that gradually grew bigger as they approached. Wim and I sprinted in the direction it appeared one of them would land, hoping to beat the Germans there. Minutes later, we were rewarded when, out of breath, we got to the spot and saw our first live American.

Standing in a field of tall grass, with soot smeared across his face and a cut profusely bleeding on his forehead, I expected he would be astonished or in shock. Instead, when he saw us fighting our way through the weeds to get to him, the American smiled and calmly lit a cigarette. By the time we were at arm's-length to him, he was smoking easily.

"Hello," the man said, grimacing a little as he smiled. His parachute was lying on the ground, still wet from the descent. Wim and I gaped at the man, unable to believe that he was acting this way in the face of what he'd just gone through. "You're not Germans, I take it?" the American asked. "I hope you'll help me. I have a few bad shrapnel wounds that need taken care of."

I immediately took out my pocket knife and cut a strip of the white silk from his chute, bandaging it to his forehead. Despite his calm demeanor, the American was in a lot of pain and couldn't walk without difficulty. Wim and I therefore placed him between us and half-walked, half-dragged him toward the nearest farm – the Holstag farm.

"We'll hide you here," Wim told the American. "Just hang on."

At the farmhouse, we sat the man down in a chair and started treating his other wounds hidden beneath his clothes. The owner of the farm came out and offered cherries, but the American refused to eat any until he watched Wim and I eat them first.

With a smile, he told us his name was Leroy Blocker from the state of Kansas. He was a sergeant and a board-gunner who had bombed the ball bearing factory near Huls in northern Germany earlier that day. Then, as he ate a handful of cherries, Blocker added, "Holland cherries are good."

Not two minutes later, we heard the sound of motorcycles. The door burst open and helmeted German soldiers stormed inside, rifles ready.

"Hands up!" they yelled. They jerked the American out of his chair, ignoring me as I tried to explain that he was wounded. Then they pushed him into one of the motor side cars and drove off, leaving Wim and me empty-handed, just staring after the trail of exhaust. The woman who'd brought the cherries started weeping. For many years afterwards, I wondered what became of that American.

In the spring of 1980 while living in Caldwell, Idaho, a new neighbor moved in and introduced himself.

"Where are you from?" I asked.

"Kansas," he replied. His name was Mr. Acheson and he had come from Topeka.

I do not know what made me ask such a wild question, but after all those years, I still remembered Blocker's name and that he'd come from Kansas. So I asked, "Does the name Blocker mean anything to you?"

After I explained myself, Mr. Acheson said, "Yes, I do know of a former blacksmith in Topeka with several sons, and one or two were in the Air Force during World War II."

My heart raced. Mr. Acheson promised to call his brother back home to find out if we were actually talking about the same person. Shortly thereafter, he brought me a letter with a telephone number and the news that Leroy was indeed still living in Kansas.

I called the number and introduced myself.

There was a short pause on the other end. Then – "Are you the Dutch boy who made the bandage from my parachute and put it on my head?"

"Yes, I was," I said.

Leroy stopped talking, for a moment emotionally overcome.

"Are you calling from Holland?" he asked.

"I immigrated to America after the war. I've lived in Idaho since 1954."

Without hesitation, Leroy immediately offered to drive to Idaho with his wife and meet up.

What a reunion we had! We had only known each other for an hour at most over thirty-five years before, yet when we saw each other again, it was as if he had once again jumped from the sky with a parachute.

Blocker told me exactly what happened after the Germans captured him: After getting hospitalized in Arnhem, he was transported to one of Germany's "luxury" Prisoner of War camps deep in Germany, called Stalag 17. He stayed there until the Russians arrived, and forced him and hundreds of other men to march off toward the West. For thirty days during the spring of '45, they marched with hardly any shelter and little food. They struggled to stay alive, and many men died on the journey. Finally, they were rescued by the American Army in April, exhausted and weak.

Leroy had more surgery when he returned home, including the complete removal of shrapnel from his head. He became the postmaster in a small town named Wetmore, Kansas.

I could not forget his unique story if I tried. It's important to remember – remember what could and did happen. Many untold stories are lost and gone forever.

Eisenhower on the Secret Radio

As the war continued to progress in the Allies' favor, we listened daily to the secret radio reports from England, even though it was strictly forbidden. The Germans had confiscated all radios in 1942, and most people complied.

But while we gave up an old radio, we kept a new one hidden in an empty cement water trough, covered with several pieces of corrugated metal sheets. Each day, we listened for news from England, knowing that the American invasion was coming – but when? And where?

As time stretched on, the Germans' restless and nervous behavior felt like electricity filling the air, lightning ready to strike at any moment. The power of an Allied Army two-and-a-half million strong lay coiled up in England, ready to spring across the channel into German-occupied France.

On the morning of June 6, 1944, the Army sprung, causing a shock-wave throughout Europe and the whole world. The largest armada in history had been assembled, including more than 5,000 ships accompanied by 4,000 small crafts. Additionally, 23,000 paratroopers had dropped behind the German beach defenses.

When we listened to the secret radio messages, we heard Supreme Commander Eisenhower's farewell to those brave men:

> Soldiers, sailors, and airmen of the Allied Expeditionary Force! You are about to embark upon the great crusade, toward which we have striven these many months. The eyes of the whole world are upon you. The hopes and prayers of liberty-loving people everywhere march with you...
> Your task will not be an easy one. Your enemy is well-trained, well-equipped, and battle-hardened.

We sat there glued to the radio; all work and activity stopped around the farm. What unbelievably good news!

The Germans around Angeren were frantic and placed orders and proclamations. Later that night, a sergeant Major announced that we all had an 8 p.m. curfew. Those who were not off the streets by that time would be shot.

I had expected the Germans to lose heart and give up, but it turned out just the opposite. They fought back ferociously, not just in our village, but in German-occupied France. It took the Allies more than a month to establish a solid inland foothold, and it was not until the end of July that they succeeded.

We soon witnessed disorganized German troops fleeing through our area towards Germany. What a pretty sight! Most villagers had been waking up every day just in order to witness this long-awaited retreat. Hitler's mighty men had transformed into a dirty and exhausted lot headed for home. They would ask in loud voices, "How far to the ferry over the Rhine River?" or "What's the name of this village?" All road signs had been removed.

The movement of men and equipment went on day and night for at least a month, and the numbers moving from town to town seemed to only increase each day. They moved all kinds of vehicles: horse-drawn and a few motorized ones with French and Belgium license plates. Most of them, however, walked on foot, carrying whatever they could, often stealing food and bikes. Some were so tired they dropped their packs and arms along the way. Others simply collapsed by the roadside.

Family Farm Bombed

On Sunday night of August 16, 1944, many bombers flew overhead. Which side they were on, I didn't know. About midnight, Wim and I saw some fighting and shooting above town. We eventually went to bed because we had seen this same thing multiple times before.

About an hour later, a neighbor awakened us, pounding on our door and yelling that our buildings for storing hay and straw had caught fire from stray bombs. We sprinted outside, but there was nothing we could do besides watch everything go up in flames, including thousands of saved-up guilders and any hopes and dreams the war hadn't stripped us of.

It was a good thing we'd run outside. Another small bomb hit our house that night. Nothing could be saved.

This loss was a terrible shock to my parents, but thankfully, nobody was hurt or killed. We temporarily moved in with a Protestant minister and his family, next to his church. It was a large, sturdy villa with fourteen rooms. At least we had a roof over our heads.

****

German soldiers of a different caliber arrived in town from Normandy during the first part of September, 1944. They were of the Panzer unit, a supposedly elite division of the German army. But the men appeared dirty and exhausted, brought with them their dead and wounded, and always traveled at night.

Sometimes, the Panzers would knock on the pastor's door to demand something be given to them, although they lacked the usual forcefulness of German soldiers. On these occasions, the pastor would delegate me to deal with the Germans, because, he said, he could not master their language well. But I think his unwillingness to handle them had more to do with his appearance: he was a small man who wore thick glasses and looked Jewish.

Late one night, two young SS officers knocked on the front door of the pastor's house. When I opened the door, these men introduced themselves properly and asked if they could borrow some blankets for the night. It was a strange request, because German soldiers usually just demanded something and then took it. I was about to agree, sensing some underlying threat in their polite manner, when the pastor's wife came to the door and rudely asked what they wanted.

"They want some blankets," I tried to explain. Before the Germans could nod in assent, though, the pastor's wife scowled and slammed the door in their faces.

I stared at her in the ringing silence.

"Do you know what you're doing?" I asked in disbelief. "They could force us out into the streets within minutes!"

Angry tears welled in her eyes. "It isn't fair," she whispered.

Knowing that I needed to fix the ugly situation before the whole household was punished, I opened the door again and apologized for the wife's behavior. I also told the Germans why my family and I were staying at the pastor's house.

"We have very little left, but you could still borrow a few blankets," I said.

One of the German officers shook his head, a small smile on his face. "Call the pastor's wife back and have *her* produce the blankets. Not you."

The tension made my hair stand on end. But when I asked the pastor's wife as calmly as I could to bring the blankets, she did so, her eyes red and averted. Breathing a sigh of relief when the German officers left, I thought we had avoided a catastrophe at the expanse of a few blankets.

But the next morning, to my surprise, the Germans returned the blankets, thanking me for lending them out. Behind the officers, I noticed that many more vehicles had arrived in the night, parked on the streets. Some trucks were filled with heaps of dead bodies.

"May we see the interior of this home?" one of the German officers asked, handing back the blankets.

Now I had to force down panic. Feigning calm, I let the two officers in, showing them the kitchens and rooms. The pastor's children peeked out from behind their parents' legs, scared; my younger sisters, all younger than fifteen, watched by my mother with timid demeanors. When the officers saw the pastor, their gaze lingered on his hair and glasses, but they said nothing about his appearance.

"Right," said one of the Germans when they were finished inspecting the house. "We have orders to evacuate you and use the house for headquarters as part of the division in town."

Silence. Both the pastor and his wife grew correspondingly red and white in the face. I scrambled to find anything I could say to prevent this from happening, but I knew that the Catholic priest across the street had already been kicked out of his home, and that German soldiers were now using it as a field hospital. There was nothing I could do.

The second officer, more as a reminder to himself rather than a plea for help, said quietly to the horrified air, "We also need help burying some men who died a few days ago. We were hoping to bury them in the cemetery by your church." He sounded miserable.

After a few seconds, Wim, in a hollow voice, volunteered to help bury the soldiers. After all, a dead man was still a dead man no matter which side of the war he was on.

Both Germans' eyes grew wide at my brother's offer; they must have suspected we would rebel rather than give agreeable help. In return for Wim's help, they reconsidered their order for us to vacate the home.

"You can stay," they said, "and continue living in *some* of the rooms. The cellar and the kitchen."

So over the next few days, German soldiers trooped in and out of the house, filthy and fatigued. We did not see much of them for long, but one of the two original German officers came quite often. His name was Lieutenant Themans, an aide de camp of General Heinz Harmel's division. He was about my age, twenty-one, with an agreeable personality despite his stance. Sometimes in a frenzy of activity, he would forget I could speak German and spit out important information to his soldiers. I also heard announcements over the German radio vehicles right outside, which I interpreted for the family.

These troops were in our town, I told my family and the pastor's family in private, to watch and protect the two large bridges over the Rhine River – one in Arnhem and the other in Nymege, spaced less than eight miles apart. Why, I still couldn't tell. But it was clear something big was about to happen.

A few days after Lieutenant Themans and his soldiers first occupied the pastor's house, I heard shooting across the street where a neighbor, Toon

Derksen, operated a café, bakery, and farm building that housed pigs and cattle. Running to the scene, I found that some of Derken's fattest pigs were being shot by the Germans. It was understandable, since those SS soldiers had been deprived of fresh meat for seven weeks of traveling through Belgium to Holland.

However, Derksen protested loudly, asking me to speak with the soldiers about restitution. I looked over to the main butcher, a big, mustached German who was sharpening knives as we spoke. I certainly did not like his looks, so I decided not to interfere. I told Derksen that even if he did receive payment for the butchered pigs, the money would be worthless.

Plus, these soldiers rarely paid or asked for what they wanted. These were visitors who cleaned and bathed stark-naked in full view. When they wanted chickens or eggs, they did not go to the owners, but directly to the chicken coops. If locks were used, civilians found them shot to pieces and chickens and eggs gone anyways. If civilians did not cooperate, they soon found themselves on the street like the Catholic Priest.

I explained this all to Derksen and walked away before any more trouble started, hoping he would understand that his pigs were not a battle worth fighting for.

The Battle of the Bridge

One man belonging to the Arnhem Resistance group occasionally swung by town to visit me. His name was Albert Horstman, and he would arrive on a small, white motorcycle with red crosses painted on the side. He was of slight build, handsome, and part-Jewish; I admired him for his daring nerve and coolness.

When Horstman came to our village one day in August of 1944, he spotted the Panzers all camouflaged in the barns or under trees. "Who are these soldiers, Gys?" he asked fearfully.

In answer, I pointed at the sides of their tanks. "Look at the small, red emblem."

Horstman's expression grew even more grave. In a hushed voice, he said, "These are the most feared enemy soldiers. What the hell are they doing *here*?"

I told Horstman that I had overheard Themans and his men talking about protecting two bridges. I presumed that an airborne attack was about to take place, in which, I knew, an Arnhem bloodbath would occur. "Do you think we should report their activity to England?" I asked. When Horstman agreed promptly, I wrote down the number of men and tanks so that he could call the headquarters of the British Army.

But alas, when Horstman called, the British, under the leadership of Marshal Montgomery, stated that Dutch Resistance reports could not be trusted.

I wish they would have listened. Thousands of lives could have been saved.

****

It only took four days of rest for the weary and dirty SS soldiers to transform into a fearsome unit again: clean, rejuvenated, and wearing black uniforms, about 200 newly-fanatic and blood-thirsty men did a passerby march.

General Heinz Harmel arrived in person and saluted them. They marched by in columns four men wide, singing deafeningly as they passed by the pastor's house. The village vibrated. Harmel stood rigid in order to salute and inspect the black-uniformed soldiers as they went by.

What a difference four days had made! A striking young officer, Heinz Brinkmann, whom I had personally met in our house, led the troops. I believe he held the rank of *oberscharrfuhrer*, or

Major. I had to admit that it was a splendid performance, even though they were our enemy. Frightening, but splendid.

A few days before September 17, the soldiers left in the middle of the night. One by one, the tanks started up and rumbled out of town, over the dike with only moonlight to guide them. I remember the silhouettes of the men sitting on top of the tanks, black figures against a star-scattered sky. Wim and I watched them disappear in the direction of a ferry that led to Pannerden.

"Good riddance," we murmured, thinking they were leaving for good.

****

On Sunday, September 17, a bright Sunday morning, we were proven wrong.

Swarms of engine planes appeared in the sky over Arnhem and released thousands of British parachutists. Bombing and anti-aircraft fire erupted around the city, so bright and loud that Wim and I could see and hear the explosions just standing on top of a dike in our village.

Hundreds of gliders flew over our own heads too, looking for places to land. As one flew above us, on fire, we heard the men inside screaming agony. It was a sickening sound.

The Germans had expected this attack. Later, we heard that the SS soldiers who'd left at midnight had traveled only about thirty miles before turning around toward the Battle of the Bridge again. The British held out for four days with only 600 men led by Colonel John Frost. They fought a heroic fight, but the American's 82nd Parachute Division that was supposed to aid them never reached the Arnhem Bridge in time. John Frost and his brave men had to surrender. Frost's tanks were destroyed one after another by German heavy armor.

The entire city of Arnhem was evacuated, left as an empty shell. Almost 100 thousand citizens had to leave, not knowing where to go or for how long. Everybody was confused and disappointed. Only a few days before, the Dutch people had sincerely thought the end of the war was approaching.

But the worst was yet to come.

Friend or Foe?

We stayed in our village for a month under heavy artillery fire and bombing. Some of the same men from the SS Frundsberg Division returned to our town, but without tanks. Instead, they brought with them all kinds of war booty: jeeps and equipment that they showed off. They displayed a new kind of haughtiness they had not previously shown, acting like children playing with new toys. They ran around with jeeps and motorcycles; they tried out the English pistols and machine guns, declaring happily that the British tools were of inferior quality.

Lieutenant Themans, though he was no longer staying in the pastor's house, told me in secret that even though the Germans had won the battle, he wasn't quite sure about the fate of the war as a whole. The quality of the British fighting had surprised him.

I had long talks with him. Even though he was my enemy, I could not make myself hate him, especially since he never raised his voice, never demanded anything of me, and always wore a sad and worn-out expression whenever he talked about the war.

Lieutenant Themans told me gruesome stories about the campaign in Russia, Sicily, and France. Everywhere the Germans went, they lost men and materials. He personally thought that the Caen battle in Normandy had been the worst. The Germans had lost almost half their men in a seven-week battle.

"And naturally," Lieutenant Themans muttered to me, "most of the replacements are young fanatics. You know, most of our SS men are under twenty years old."

Though extremely dangerous for Lieutenant Themans to confide in me, I think he just wanted someone to talk to besides his own men. Or perhaps he saw the possibility of defeat for the mighty German Army barreling down upon him. But for whatever reason, this hardened SS enemy officer respected and trusted me – in fact, I suspected, he respected the Dutch people as a whole. Talking to me was his only way of showing reverence to all of my people at once.

He told me that the German Viking Division had almost been annihilated by Rostov and Kiev in Russia. That is why several of my friends who'd joined the Nazis had never returned home – they'd believed in the free National-Socialist Party as a means of improving the lives of the working class. They had believed in the seemingly high ideals of National Socialism and Germany's economic recovery. The world-shaking military propaganda had inspired them to sign up for the elite SS, only to find their demise on the endless Russian steppes.

Lieutenant Themans also told me about anti-Jewish atrocities committed in concentration camps. By now, I had heard rumors of mass killing camps, but I had never believed them to be true. The prospect of human annihilation, of members of one species turning on each other in such ghastly and destructive ways, had been too cruel of an idea for me to believe.

But hearing those words come from a German SS officer's mouth, I was stunned. Themans himself had been offered a job as a special SS guard with the "privilege" of working in those death camps as a Nazi, but he had declined. Hearing that, I respected him even more for his refusal of bribery.

****

Staying in the pastor's house instead of Themans was a mean SS sergeant named Frits, who did most of his cooking on our own kitchen stove. He had been everywhere possible in the war, and had been wounded 36 times. When he took off his shirt, it looked like a living map of all his healed wounds and scars.

Frits was crippled and handicapped, but twice as fanatic. Sometimes he barked orders for me to fetch meat or liver from dying animals or to go gather onions from farmers. He and his officers loved liver and onions. They had also brought a whole truckload of stolen food and wares from Arnhem, including barrels full of butter. Once, an officer brought to the house three good-looking French girls to entertain them.

After the battle of Arnhem, however, Frits brought back a 15-year-old Russian boy named Nicolaas. No girls this time. The Germans used him for kitchen chores and washing, mistreating him terribly. My mother and sisters felt so sorry for the boy that they cried when he was beaten.

Nicolaas must have been from a good family somewhere in Russia. He was well-mannered and could play the piano and sing beautifully. Sometimes my family came up from the cellar, into the kitchen just to listen to him. His voice and the piano keys would create a music that took us away, if only for a few moments, from the war entirely.

That is, until Frits stormed in and demanded more liver.

****

One afternoon, American bombers dropped heavy bombs on our village and about fifty people were killed. One bomb fell hardly thirty yards from the minister's house. The church tower next to us swayed, and everything shook violently, but Lieutenant Themans instructed everybody with amazing calmness. Themans had not been thinking about himself during this crisis. This event greatly impressed me.

A few days later, we had a chat together in a U.S. jeep late at night. It was raining outside, the water bringing the stench of smoke and ash to the ground, refreshing the world. Themans sat behind the wheel and unexpectedly asked what I thought the outcome of the war would be.

Without hesitation, I answered, "Unless some secret weapon that everyone is talking about is employed – Germany will lose."

Themans was quiet for a long time, but finally agreed with me.

"I don't believe in secret weapons anymore," he said. Then I heard him whisper, "This damned war." And bending forward, he started to weep.

I did not say a word, but let the SS officer cry in silence as the rain drummed on the American windshield. And as I saw his tears land on the steering wheel, I no longer knew whether he was a friend or an enemy.

I don't think I will ever know.

Meeting a Mustang Pilot

On September 19, while a dogfight caused the air to explode with bombs and gunshots, a pilot, whether friend or foe, bailed out of a P-51 Mustang in a parachute. While descending with his open chute, a German plane fired on him, so I guessed he was American.

I did not think this pilot had any chance to hide, let alone escape. The Germans were everywhere, swarming across Angeren in every nook and cranny. Therefore, I did not go near the place he had landed – too often I had rushed toward a descending pilot only to find the Germans already there, taking him hostage or putting a bullet in his head. Better not to witness more than I had to.

Four more planes came down that day. When a bomb struck a nearby farm, thirty-seven people were killed and many more wounded. German soldiers and evacuees from Arnhem and other nearby towns had sought shelter on that farm. They found death instead.

My friends and I helped identify the victims after dousing the fire. Our duty was to sort out limbs and body parts and gather them if possible. While occupied with this gruesome task, recognizing several faces, a neighbor girl rode up to me on her bicycle. Her name was Truus Kempkes.

Whispering in my ear, she said, "Come with me. I know where the American pilot is."

I quietly slipped after Truus. We drew close to a tobacco patch, where German soldiers were searching for the pilot with rifles and machine pistols. I decided to wait until dark to try to find him, so leaving Truus, I returned to my task of identifying dead victims. Instead of deliberating on all the faces I recognized, I thought about the possible rescue of the hidden American pilot. Even if I found him in the dark, I wondered, what should be done with him and where I should take him?

All through the evening, the gunfire and screams never ceased.

****

That night, I approached the crash site in total darkness. All of my friends in the Resistance were fighting fires – a haystack that had caught fire from burning pieces of a plane, a house that had caught fire from a bomb. When I asked some of the men who were not preoccupied to help me retrieve the American pilot, they said no and hurried away, their eyes flickering nervously around for signs of the Germans. I soon realized this was a task I would have to do alone.

Quietly, I came to the field of tobacco leaves. I did not notice any guards or scouts, only a large hole in the ground and plane debris scattered all about. Relieved that the Germans had given up, I softly whistled the V-code several times: "tha tha tha-thaaa" – it was the same tune that always bonged right before secret BBC messages. I also whispered out into the empty air that I was a friend trying to help. Nothing happened.

I spoke again. "American, I am your friend."

It occurred to me that this American was either a very cautious man or badly wounded. He had successfully evaded the Germans so far, but it was likely that those helmeted soldiers with machine pistols would find him eventually if I failed to locate him now. This was my only chance to help.

As I resumed my search, the fires from burning buildings near the Rhine Bridge lit up the sky. In the light, I saw something moving toward me. A man – tired-looking and weak – hobbled up to me from under some bushes near a ditch. My heart jumped into my throat in an indescribable moment of relief and amazement.

He shook my hand and after our introduction, showed me his pistol. It was a special model 45, which I definitely did not want. I told him to keep it close, for he may need to use it himself. I myself always carried a sharp knife in a scabbard for emergencies.

My first priority was to get away from the crash area as quickly as possible. We snuck to a large nearby farm, one of the biggest around. With its large outbuildings and home, it was a good choice for a hiding place.

"These people who live here will be your friends," I told the American as I rang the doorbell anxiously.

The owner, Mr. A Emmerzaal, let us inside. Once under proper lamplight, I could see that the young American stood about six feet tall and was handsome with black hair and dark eyes. He said his name was Lieutenant Howard Moebius and he had been stationed in England. He spoke calmly with a strong voice, and his flight suit impressed us all. For him to still be alive after such an ordeal was a miracle. Also, I must admit, we all admired him even more after he doled out cigarettes and chocolate bars from his many pockets. But I was still tense.

Two attractive young girls evacuated from a farm near the Waal Bridge were living in the house and wanted to claim the American right then and there. I took Mr. Emmerzaal aside, asking if he could possibly hide the American for a few days.

His answer shocked me.

"No," he said, his voice lowered but firm. "I've been hiding enough people around here. And he's an *American*, Gys. Those are the Germans' worst enemies. If they find a few Dutch kids living under this roof, they'd do nothing more than threaten me, perhaps turn them out of the house. If they find *him* here…"

Not wanting to hear more or show the disgust on my face, I left Mr. Emmerzaal and tried to explain to the pilot that unfortunately, he couldn't stay here. Instead, I thought it best to hide him for a few days on my old farm, where a two-room apple shed still stood a quarter mile from my old home. A few weeks earlier, this shed had housed three German deserters and two Belgium labor deserters, but they had all disappeared. Before vanishing, however, they had managed to dig a deep, cellar-like hole for protection.

I do not know if Meobius understood me completely, for my English was clipped and he knew virtually no Dutch. But he followed me easily when I led him outside, through fields and over ditches and fences instead of the main road. All these things were familiar to me, even in the dark of night.

As we neared the apple shed, we noticed the door open. To my disappointment, German voices were issuing, rough and loud, from inside. Carefully retreating, I whispered to Moebius that we would go to the pastor's home where I lived. We passed by the ruins of my family's farm and home – how I wished that they were still intact!

Nearing the pastor's home, I looked at the church next to it about fifty paces away. An idea came to me: we could sleep in the church tower and think of something better the next day.

I asked the pilot to wait outside in the garden while I went inside to talk to my mother and brothers. Frits and other radio signalmen were upstairs, so in private I told my family about the American and my plans to spend the night in the church tower. I just needed the church key from the pastor.

"He'll never hand that key over," one of my sisters, Lucie, said.

But I went upstairs and asked the pastor anyways. He refused.

Heat boiled up within me. "Listen," I said. "I've had enough opposition from my own countrymen. This American trusts me, and he needs me. He already fooled the Germans once, he can do it again. Which side are you on, anyways, if you don't help? Any true enemy of Hitler would help Germany's worst enemy, America. Are you not a true enemy of Hitler?"

"Of course I am," the pastor stammered.

"Then I need the key."

Eyes trained on my face, looking disturbed, the pastor reached within his pocket and produced the key, putting it in my hands.

I thanked him, giving a nod.

Grabbing two blankets – the same ones Lieutenant Themans had once borrowed – I snuck the American pilot into the church tower and told him I'd stay with him for the night. I did not expect to sleep much, but it felt safe with a thick, oak church door locked and bolted between us and the Germans.

Surprisingly, the pilot went straight to sleep on the top floor of the church tower, leaving just enough room for us to both lie down. Wide awake, I heard him talk in his sleep and make noises as if a nightmare he couldn't escape was tormenting him. I supposed he was *living* a nightmare, being shot down and in a strange country with nowhere to go but a church attic.

The Germans' monotonous marching down below on the streets halted on the dike road close to the church. I could hear the horses pulling some of the vehicles snort, glad for a rest. Soldiers' voices became louder and louder as they headed for the church, perhaps seeking shelter. My pulse quickened. When the soldiers found the door locked, they pounded on it with the butts of their rifles.

The hollow, eerie noise awakened Moebius. He sat up, and we listened with bated breaths as the hammering faltered.

Then we heard them headed for a neighbor's, Toon Derksen's café, where they made even more ruckus, repeatedly banging on the doors, but to no avail.

From the dike road we heard a loud voice hollering into the still night, *"Heinrich lass die schwein hunde schlafen wirgehen weiter*!" Heinrich, let the son of a bitch sleep on, we have to go!

Then they left with a "clunk, clunk" sound. One of their wagons had a flat tire.

After this, Moebius drifted back to sleep. Leaving my blanket behind, I stole out of the church, looking for a better and safer place for him to hide. It was about 4 a.m. when I ran into Antoon Stevens, the village policeman. We knew each other well and he was aware of my Resistance work – he had even offered to help several times in the past. In an undertone, I told him who was in the attic of the church as we spoke, hoping against hope that I could trust him.

I was rewarded. Minutes later, I ran back to the attic, awoke Moebius, and whispered to him to follow me. We made our way through the fields again until we came to the policeman's door. Once the pilot was safe inside, I went back home, exhausted, but relieved – and happy. An American Mustang pilot had successfully slipped right under the Germans' noses.

For now, he was safe.

Saving Sherwood

The next day, September 20, one of Frits's radio signal men came rushing downstairs, asking me if I had heard that the British were losing the battle of the Arnhem Rhine Bridge. He added excitedly that the German SS troops were slaughtering them all. But, he said, the "*Die verdammte Americanen*" had taken the Waal Bridge by Nymegen with thousands of casualties on both sides. Our village and the area between the two rivers would become a fighting zone, he predicted.

The radio signalman was right. Heavy artillery pieces soon rolled into town. Even north of the Rhine River, Germans shot over our town toward the Allied troops near Nymegen, firing their canons repeatedly and shaking the houses. Before long, we would receive heavy firing from the Allied frontline in return. One man always took up position in the church tower during the day to serve as a lookout – the same spot Moebius and I had slept.

It became dangerous just to step outside. All stores and bakeries had closed down. Dead and dying cattle lay everywhere on the streets, and nobody could take ten steps without passing a poorly-dug human grave. If anyone was seen after 8 p.m. he would find himself in one of these graves before the night's end.

Thankfully, Lieutenant Themans had supplied me with a special *Ausweis*, a permit with his signature and SS stamp. The 8 p.m. curfew no longer applied to me.

Using this permit one night, I visited a young man named Casper Janssen, the son of a factory owner. He was about eighteen, artistic, and eager to help me for a good cause. With a picture that Moebius had given me, he carefully made the American pilot a false ID card, his handwriting the exact replica of a real printed version. He had to do his work by hand, he said, because the Germans had taken away his typewriter the day before.

****

Before I could give Moebius his ID card, my sisters and Wim told me that a seventeen-year-old Dutch boy, while loading a horse cart, had been hit by a stray bullet earlier that day.

"Well," said Wim, "It was either a bullet or a flying piece of metal from a pilot's plane that the Germans struck. British plane, I think. The pilot tried to belly land, but I don't know if he was successful or not, I just know that pieces of metal were flying everywhere and could have easily killed someone standing on the streets."

Wim needed help loading the young boy to take him to his parents. The boy's name was Kobus Romein, and he had helped us often on the farm.

Shortly after the boy had been buried, a friend of ours, Hent van Deelen, arrived at the pastor's house to say that the British Spitfire pilot had survived his belly-landing crash, but was wounded. Feeling exactly as I had when I'd set out to save Moebius, I followed Deelen on bicycle to the site and we viewed from a distance several Germans with rifles, already searching. I waited on top of a haystack for several hours until the Germans left. Then I went alone to find the British pilot while van Deelen went searching for civilian clothes.

Unlike with Moebius, I spotted this pilot without having to whistle the V code. He was a small man hiding under some bushes in a ditch, for some reason staring into a fruit jar full of water.

Wondering what in the world he was doing, I whistled the V code just to relay that I was friendly. The pilot understood and was not scared. He crawled out of the brambles, attempting to smile, and introduced himself as Douglas Sherwood. He was not a British as Wim had assumed, but a Canadian Captain in the R.A.F.

He looked awful. In the crash, Sherwood's plane had struck the ditch and his face had slammed into his scope sight. His right eye was badly swollen, his nose bent at a wrong angle, obviously broken.

"I was trying to use the fruit jar as a mirror to see what I looked like," Sherwood explained, unable to speak without spitting out a mouthful of blood. Producing a small signal mirror so that he could see his reflection, I knew that if I didn't find this man a doctor soon, it would not matter that he had evaded the Germans. Nobody can hide from death in ditch brambles – and this Canadian looked as if he wouldn't be able to survive very long without some serious help.

Because Sherwood could not walk on his own, I told him we must wait until dark to transport him to safety. That night, as severe grenade and machine gunfire erupted all around us, a man named Willy Linden and I carried Sherwood several miles to a neighbor's shed. Several times, Willy and I could have sworn the Germans spotted us, because we were right by the frontline and the firing would get so intense, it sometimes missed us by only inches. When this happened, we laid low to wait for calm.

Finally, we placed Sherwood on the floor in the neighbor's shed. I told the pilot I would be back with a doctor and sped off on my bicycle to the Resistance's go-to doctor in another town.

But Dr. Braun refused to come. When I explained that a Canadian was dying in a shed, he lifted up his sleeve to reveal serious lash marks and other scars covering his skin from elbow to wrist.

"Don't you remember, Gys?" he asked.

Dr. Braun had been beaten and tortured the last time he had helped a German's enemy.

So I bicycled back to town and arrived at the door of Sister Thye instead, a known nurse. This brave lady came to Sherwood's aid immediately, no matter the deadly risks involved. She was a hero in her own right.

Besides his eye and nose, Sherwood's right knee was badly bruised. She told me it would take several days before he could walk.

Before long, however, Sherwood was begging, "Help me escape as soon as possible."

When I finally delivered Moebius's false ID card and told him about Sherwood, he suggested bringing the Canadian through the fighting lines to the Waal River, to the liberated area. Moebius knew the map of our vicinity as well as I did, and drew a route for us. He was amazing!

Suitable clothes were found for Sherwood, but he refused to take off his flight suit. On September 30, Sherwood and I walked three miles in plain daylight, Sherwood carrying a basket full of apples for his trip. The roadsides were occupied by Germans in foxholes with machine guns in many places. Sherwood, who had never seen a German soldier up close before, began sweating terribly as we passed them.

Once, I thought he was right behind me, but when I turned around found Sherwood several yards behind, actually handing apples out to the Germans.

What are you doing? I wanted to ask, fear clouding my mind. The purpose of walking in daylight was to act as casual as possible in order to attract the least amount of attention we could!

But to my surprise, the German soldiers seemed so grateful for the simple apple that they accepted the fruit with a nod and a smile. When we finally got to a brick factory where some of my Resistance friends were waiting to take Sherwood on, his basket was nearly empty. Yet the man himself smiled as we parted ways.

Help from an SS Doctor

I urged Moebius to do the same as Sherwood – sneak out of Holland with help from the Resistance. But he refused, expecting to be liberated within a few a days.

On October 6, a lone, two-engine Martin bomber on a photo mission flew over the pastor's house – on fire. The Germans around us jumped for joy, a jeep immediately headed for where the plane would land.

Before Wim or I could as much as move, we saw three pilots bail out. Then, with a loud explosion, the plane burst into pieces, one engine falling into the third airman's parachute and hurtling him to the ground. The terrible fate of this young American stood out to us over the numerous other deaths… for the Germans found his body on our old farm.

The other two crew members drifted toward roughly the same area. When the Germans found them all dead, burned alive, they came grumbling back, no longer interested. But a few days later, Wim and I scouted the area, and found two bodies lying close to the wreckage next to our plow, which had stood in the field since the battles started. The dead crewmen were named Edward Sadula and Norman Truax. The third we did not find until eight months later when we plowed the field after the war. His name was Sergeant George Boyer from Coalville, Utah.

The bodies of the first two lay there for several days, pilfered of boots and valuables. So I went to a German SS field doctor to ask permission to bury the pilots. The young doctor offered to go with me. We rode bicycles to the scene of the two bodies. The Allies must have spotted us from a distance because intense artillery and machine gun fire erupted all around us. We were forced to dive into ditches seven times before we reached the town again. The doctor told me to bury them in the dark.

"And come to me again if you ever need anything else," he said. This doctor, young as he was, must have had immense battle experience, for he had been more than calm when so near death. Both of our bicycles were riddled with bullet holes.

Surprisingly the next day, this same doctor toured the town with other SS men in a yellow convertible car, waving at me happily as he went by. Apparently, he and his friends had had more than enough to drink.

Lieutenant Themans, too, would sometimes appear on my doorstep with wine and ham. This was the life of the front-line soldier – one day in grave danger, the next day happy and half-drunk with war booty.

Once, Themans came reeling to me and asked in a drawling voice, "Do you know where the pastor is? I need a pear." He hiccupped; I could smell the alcohol on his breath. "Prayer, I mean."

"No, I don't where he is, Themans," I said firmly, even though the pastor was in the house as we spoke. Themans cursed good-naturedly and staggered away.

After this episode, we did not see much more of the SS men. They left to fight elsewhere. Frits, too, went stomping away, and a more peaceful German artillery crew replaced him and his men. When things quieted down during the evenings, my mother and family would emerge from the cellar. The new German soldiers living in our house needed some relaxation, so their Lieutenant, a man named Harms, would play the piano like Nicolaas used to. Mother would sometimes ask the soldiers to sing, and their voices would melt together beautifully. One of my little sisters, Willie, would sing along, her sweet voice joining in perfect harmony.

In the darkest of times, when the mixture of units in our town would come back from the front line every day tired, hungry, and dragging the dead with them, there were lights of hope. Lieutenant Harms was the son of a Protestant pastor, so he would lead his men in hymns and prayers. Even though the words were in German, our own pastor and my family would come upstairs and join.

Mr. Roos, the head of the Protestant's school in Angeren, lived across the street from us. He and his family of three children had survived the terrible bombing in Rotterdam, yet despite their horrors still risked continuing a two-room school. Mr. Roos often came to talk to my family and see how we were doing.

One day, his wife came to me and asked me desperately to bring back a doctor from the next town. Mr. Roos was sick and would otherwise die without certain medication. However, Doctor Braun, the same doctor who had refused to help Sherwood, also denied helping or coming with me to even *look* at the teacher.

Remembering the young SS doctor, I went to see if he could supply the medicine. The doctor telephoned a larger, SS military field hospital in Huissen, a neighboring village, and ordered a prescription for me to pick up.

I rode over the dike on my bicycle. It was a risky errand; I was shot at several times, but I brought the medicine. Mr. Roos was intensely grateful and survived the war.

When I came back to the pastor's house that night, a carload of German officers was sitting by the front steps. As I walked by, I caught a few words about how Angeren would soon be evacuated. We had heard rumors about evacuation before, but had always hoped to be liberated before that happened.

That afternoon, Bart ten Bosch, the man my sister Luci was engaged to, visited us. He was a short, strong man who came to our village by crossing the Rhine with artillery men in a rowboat, then walking the rest of the way. He often brought food, especially for my mother. She was deteriorating quickly from malnutrition, and needed eggs or other protein-rich foods that would give her strength.

This time, Bart himself looked awful. He could barely walk. He had gotten in a fight with some German soldiers who'd tried to rob him. Bart's old neighbors had entrusted him with a sum of money to keep safe. He always carried that money with him in a leather billfold with a chain around his neck. The Germans never got the money, but they had beaten him to a pulp, kicking him repeatedly in the kidneys. He urinated blood.

Since no other doctor was available in the town, I took Bart with me to the SS doctor. He arranged for me to pick up pills for Bart the next day. When I delivered the pills to Bart's farm, I discovered him lying on a pile of hay in a cow barn. Germans occupied the front living quarters of Bart's barn. He was in bad shape, but he survived the war, although he died at an early age after several kidney operations.

Bart was just another innocent victim of war.

Evacuation

On October 13, 1944, the Germans finally forced my family and the pastor's family to evacuate so that they could take over the house as an operation center. A few days later, the rest of Angeren was forced to evacuate as well.

Field gendarmes went from house to house telling everybody to leave within the next two hours. Two artillery men in our house – George and Otto – immediately offered to assist my family out of Angeren. The men rowed my loved ones in their own rowboats across the Rhine to Bart's farm. Bart met them on the other side of the river with a horse and buggy.

Meanwhile, our wagon was loaded with household goods from not just my family, but several other families as well. I was supposed to take the wagon the long way over around Pannerden Ferry. I said goodbye to my mother, father, and siblings, wondering if we would ever meet again. They all cried as they departed with George and Otto through the polder pasture toward the Rhine.

I had obtained a nice, stout horse to pull the wagon, one I knew could handle the heavy load by itself. I traveled the opposite way of the chaotic tide of people headed toward the river ferry. Some shouted at me, "Where do you think you're going?" But most were too focused on transporting themselves and their remaining property using bicycles, baby buggies, wheelbarrows, or backpacks. Livestock was running loose, German soldiers were here and there barking orders, people were burying goods they could not take along. Some who had means of transportation hurriedly butchered their livestock and loaded the fresh meat. Older people broke down and cried; I saw one old, gray-bearded man sink to his knees, praying and crying.

When he saw me through a stream of tears, he asked, "Are we ever coming back, van Beek?"

"I don't know," I said quietly.

Stevens had asked me to take all of his possessions on my wagon as well, so on my way out of town I stopped by his house. There, I took Moebius aside and asked him to come with me. "You could just act like a Dutch, leading a horse or a cow," I urged.

Moebius shook his head. "I don't want to bring any danger to you or your family," he said. Then he clapped a hand on my shoulder. "Plus, I still believe liberation is in the near future. I'm staying, Gys."

I decided to stay with Moebius that night and find him a proper hiding place in the morning. Finding some food and camouflaging the wagon, we and twelve other people – mostly those too sick and aging to do any more walking for the day – found refuge in a small house behind Steven's place, where an older couple named the Vermeulens had used to live. Stevens himself was among those who stayed. The fourteen of us huddled together in the old house as the town emptied, turning barren.

About 6 a.m. the next morning, I went outside in the pitch dark to pull some hay for my stout wagon horse. All at once, SS soldiers jumped me, rifles poking my ribs, ordering me to put my hands in the air.

"*Spion, spion!*" they bellowed.

Seizing me roughly, they dragged me to their headquarters at Stevens' house, where they questioned me angrily for hours. When I failed to give them information they wanted, they knocked me unconscious from behind.

For how long I was out, I don't know. By the time I came to, the taste of coppery blood filled my mouth, and my tongue probed some loose teeth in my gums. My pockets had been emptied except for my Ausweis.

Then I noticed Lieutenant Themans in the room, standing over me in amazement.

"Gys," he said as I blinked up at him. "What have you done?"

Spitting out blood, I explained that I'd simply been feeding a horse I was planning to use as a means of evacuating the town. In an undertone, so that the rest of the Germans could not hear, I told him about Moebius and all of the old people hiding out with me.

Lieutenant Themans looked at me long and hard. He was in a situation where he had to act as my foe rather than confident, but still, he could not seem to come up with any words.

Finally, he said, "You have two hours, Gys. Two hours to leave town, you and everyone with you."

I scrambled away, back to the old house where everyone stared at me in astonishment and horror. Telling them all we needed to hurry, I took Moebius to a shed in our apple orchard, where some Germans had left blankets and a shelter in the ground. There, I said goodbye to my dear American friend and left him with some food. I promised I would come back as soon as possible if the area was not liberated like he still believed it would be.

Soon, the rest of the elderly people, Stevens, and I were on our way with the heavy wagon, the very oldest ones riding on the wagon itself. We made our way through the ghostly town. The only person we saw was our grocery store owner and baker, Mrs. Holleman. She and some others had been forced to stay in order to bake the Germans bread when needed. When she saw me passing, Mrs. Holleman took me aside and offered an unbelievable 100 pound sack of sugar. I told her the wagon was already overloaded. But on second thought, I said, "Actually, I'll put it on the driver's seat and walk. Thank you so much, Mrs. Holleman. How much is it worth?"

"Not to worry, Gys," she said, sounding only weary and a bit sad. "You can pay for it after the war."

Thanking her again, we went on. We had to use the dike road since the normal route was pocketed with large craters, but the dike road's incline was chewed up by heavy tanks as well. My horse, so big and strong, started to falter. I began pushing on her flank from behind, trying to help. A few of the other people, including Stevens, tried helping me, too. But even with all of our effort combined, my horse couldn't go any further.

"Okay everyone," I said, wiping sweat and dried blood from my brow. "Stay put until I come back with help."

I jogged back down the incline toward the pastor's house once more, heading straight into the mouth of the trap. But I was hoping to find a vehicle. At the pastor's house, I saw two jeeps and – just stepping out of the front door as I approached – Themans. He had tried "looking" for me at my old house.

Once more, astonishment clouded Theman's face at the sight of me as my old boxer dog jumped on me, happy to see me after several days.

Before he could even open his mouth, I grabbed my boxer and said, "I'll trade you her for one of your Tommy jeeps." He had always joked about one day stealing the dog because he was so fond of her.

Themans blinked. Then, he let out a roar of laughter, clutching his stomach and shaking.

"You've got guts, my friend, haven't you?" he choked. "C'mon, Gys."

He good-naturedly jumped in one of the jeeps with the dog and me and headed up the dike. With the help of the jeep a cable fastened to the wagon, the horse was able to pull us up the dike road. Everybody was relieved and thanked Lieutenant Themans.

"Goodbye, Emma," I told my dog, but Themans shook his head.

"Keep her. Consider the jeep a gift from me to you."

I shook my head, laughing, and thanked him. We said goodbye, not knowing it was the last time we'd see each other, although perhaps that was for the best. Looking back, I know Themans was considered my enemy, but he was a good man. He had proven it time and time again, and his last act – letting me keep my own dog – settled the matter once and for all. I'm glad I knew him, if only for a little while.

****

The elderly people and I continued traveling toward the ferry, where several allied fighter planes flew low overhead. We hoped and prayed that the pilots would recognize us as civilians and not shoot us.

A long line of people was ahead of us, moving slowly, and troops were continually passing because they had the right of way. The more I thought about Moebius, the worse I felt. It would take a long time before we reached the ferry, and an even longer time for me to double back for him. Forming a plan in my mind, I pulled Stevens aside.

"I want to go back and fetch Moebius," I said. "Once we're over the river, it'll be too hard to come back to the fighting area. It shouldn't take more than a day, so if you could just keep everyone in line until I get back –"

"No." Stevens had tensed up while I was talking. Now, he donned his police badge from an interior pocket and pinned it to his chest for the first time in weeks. "You need to stay put," he said. "It would be too dangerous to go back now."

"But Moebius –" I tried to argue.

In one, swift movement, Stevens jabbed his pistol into my chest. "I'm still in charge, Gys! And I say you stay. Alright?"

Slowly, I nodded. I did not know Stevens' motives, but I think he was scared. Up until that point, I had considered him a hero.

Hoping to eventually rid myself of Stevens and the other neighbors, I continued toward the ferry. Coming to a homemade ferry, I was approached by a mean-looking German sergeant.

"Give me your bike," he said.

I stared at him. My bicycle was tied behind the wagon with a rope.

"Here," I said, bringing out my papers signed by Lieutenant Themans. "My bike isn't to be taken under any circumstances."

A strong argument ensued. The sergeant started untying the bicycle from the rope; I retied it firmly. He grew so angry that he started foaming at the mouth, and the other soldiers had to urge the sergeant to back off. I wasn't worth it, they said. So I kept the bike.

On the second day's travel, I met a young man from my town on the north side of the river. He told me the whereabouts of my parents on a farm in Velp. Stevens and his family wanted to go to their friends near Apeldoorn, so we finally went our separate ways.

When I set foot on the farm where my family was staying, my father was waiting for me on the side of the highway, where he had stationed himself as lookout for me for several days. When we embraced, he said in my ear gruffly, "I knew you would come today. Your brother Jan will be excited to see you."

"Jan's back?" I asked.

"He came knocking on our door the day before yesterday."

It was wonderful to reunite with my family, but the thought of Moebius still tinged my mind with dark thoughts. I had to go back for him; I could see no liberation in his future.

I hopped on my bicycle once again and headed back. But arriving at the ferry the next day, the mean sergeant remembered me and screamed at me, "If I ever see you again, I'll shoot you!" His knuckles, white and trembling, enclosed around his rifle, and he wouldn't let me across the river.

I decided to go back to Velp and try to obtain a vehicle. Once again, I met up with Albert Horstman, the half-Jewish Resistance member with the motorcycle. He and his driver, Ceesvan

Teefelen, offered go to with me back to Angeren in a Red Cross van. The next morning, ten days after leaving my village originally, we went back to no-man's land. The van was an old truck powered with a wood and gas generator with red crosses painted on the side.

This time, we crossed the ferry without a problem. My own personal bully sergeant was not there, although a few military men helping gather cattle were.

It was uncanny to be back in Angeren with the town taking fire from the Allies' frontline. Coming to the ruins of my farm, I asked the driver to stop and let me out to investigate. Some Germans had a heavy machine gun nest in our front yard between rose bushes.

One of the soldiers, a sergeant whom I had met before, came out of the ruins of my house and met me halfway, a few of his fellow soldiers following behind him. They all knew I had once belonged on Brouwershof, and seemed relaxed without any firing going on in the immediate vicinity.

"Why'd you come back?" the sergeant called.

"I'm looking for some young, registered Holstein bulls," I lied easily, pulling out my papers and showing it to the sergeant.

He hardly glanced at it before telling me to go ahead and look around, but return soon.

It was just the break I needed. I headed toward the orchards, where I had left Moebius in the barn – although that had been ten days prior. Anything could have happened since then.

When I came to the barn, all was quiet. No Moebius. I hollered and whistled, but there was no sign of life. Disappointment flooded through me! I looked around for any messages, any clues, anything... and spotted fresh carvings on an upright beam:

M – 16, 17, 18, 19, 20, 21, 22, 23, 24

I knew then that Moebius had been in the shed up until three days before. But where was he now?

Puzzled, I walked back to my two friends in the truck with my head down. I felt low, trying to figure out what to do next, when suddenly a thunderous voice started shouting from behind me.

A large, older German was running my way, gesturing and making noise. I waited calmly for him to draw close, and then asked him, "*Was ist loss*?" What's the matter?

The German acted terribly upset, asking in a tirade of words what I was doing in the fighting area. All the while, he jabbed me with his rifle, sending little aches of pain through my ribs. After four and a half years of war and Resistance fighting, my self-control and composure had been tested often. I forced myself to listen peacefully, and most importantly, to look the wild German in the eye. Any sign of fear or insecurity, I knew, might be my end.

The German was not in the least bit interested in my papers. Perhaps he could not read. Calmly, although with a hint of authority, I said, "I have as much business to be here as you do, Soldier. If not more. Not only is this my country, but this is my farm. I was only looking for cattle. You are way out of line right now."

The German poked me in the ribs with his rifle again. "*I'm* in charge right now," he hissed. "*I* round up the livestock running around, not you." Then he ordered me to put my hands up, stating that I was his prisoner now and that I must start rounding up cattle for him.

"I have no intention of doing that," I said, my voice as composed as ever.

Somehow, slowly, I got the German to calm down – perhaps because I never raised my voice. When he told me, rather grudgingly, that he was from Armenia, I understood his abnormal behavior. Volunteers from other occupied countries were often more dangerous than the Germans. Excuse or no excuse, however, I was glad to get away from him, back to the vehicle and my friends.

"What's wrong?" Horstman asked me when he noticed my face. I told him and Ceesvan Teefelen about the carvings, and that the American pilot was gone. We thought he may have gone into town, so we circled Angeren, but to no avail. All we saw were Germans loading up cattle and hogs. The little town had an eerie stillness. There were many homes with broken windows and curtains flapping in the wind.

It was an awful, deep-pitted feeling to have to return to Velp without retrieving what I'd come for. On the way back to the ferry, the van jumping over juts and rocks in the road, we discussed the episode of the Armenian.

"I had a similar experience with a crazy German soldier 'round October 23rd, I think," Horstman said. "It was in this same area... while heading to the brick factory."

I paused. "What were you doing at the brick factory on October 23rd?"

Horstman hesitated. But then he said, "I helped haul out two pilots to the ferry for escape. A British and a Canadian."

I paused. "Did the name of the Canadian happen to be Sherwood?"

"Yes," Horstman looked surprised. "Did you know him?" I told him that I had brought Sherwood to the brick factory and I presumed him to be long gone to the liberated area.

"Well, he is now," replied Horstman.

We arrived at the ferry and encountered the same mean sergeant who wanted my bike. Unfortunately, the truck would not start when we tried to speed away. Remembering my face, the sergeant exploded with anger. He ordered us to stand with our hands up.

He and his fellow soldiers searched the truck carefully, even looking underneath it. When they found nothing valuable or exciting, they helped us push the truck off the ferry, glad to be rid of the stinking contraption, and told us to never come back.

"That was the same bastard we had trouble with on the 23rd," Horstman grumbled, glaring back as we drove onward.

"I'm not surprised," I said, almost laughing.

Back in Velp, I noticed my mother's worsening condition. Since she was packed with dozens of other misplaced people, my family immediately went about trying to find better quarters and food. After much searching, we found an old couple who agreed to take us in. Almost every other home in Velp was full of evacuees, but this kind, old couple, Mr. and Mrs. Goedheer, offered a better place to stay in all respect.

We lived there until the war's end.

A Red-Haired Paratrooper

In Velp, I was asked twice to help transport British paratroopers who were in hiding. They needed moved to a gathering place in order to return safely over the Rhine and join the Allies south of the river.

The plan was for me to transport one of the paras on the back of my bike through the empty city of Arnhem to Oosterbeek, where Resistance members gathered just west of Arnhem.

On December 3, 1944, I met this paratrooper at a secret residence. Not only was the young man vibrantly red-haired, but he wore a red mustache with points. If we got stopped by German soldiers, he was a dead-giveaway, so I told him the mustache had to come off before I would move him.

He was a small, wiry man who seemed nervous and flighty, glancing to and fro as if he thought a German would pop out from around a corner at any moment. I couldn't blame him. He had gone through hell as a prisoner, getting beaten and tortured, but had managed to escape. I told him to remain calm and stay close to me no matter what. We put him in civilian clothes, cut off his ginger mustache, and took off on the bike. It was still daylight, but sometimes that worked to our advantage, for German soldiers weren't as suspicious in the light of day. Plus, we had false papers for the para in case we got halted at a checkpoint. Once before in Arnhem, I was checked by two older soldiers who'd barely glanced at the papers before letting me go on.

On the way to Oosterbeek, a Dutch policeman approached us on a bike. Without warning, the little Brit jumped off my bike and sprinted for the woods. The black-uniformed policeman greeted me kindly and asked, as if we were merely talking about the weather, "Who just fled into the trees, may I ask?"

Deciding to tell the truth, I explained what I was doing. Thankfully, the Dutchman was not surprised. We both walked to the edge of the woods.

"Come out, Trooper!" I shouted. "It's just a Dutch. He's going to let us continue!"

"And I won't turn you in!" the policeman called, amused.

Together, we coaxed the paratrooper back out into the open. Meekly, he complimented the policeman on his "smart" uniform. It was the first time I ever heard the word smart used in that way before.

After unloading the British para at the Resistance domicile, I never saw him again. But before we parted ways, he thanked me, felt in his pocket, and handed me a small picture of him and his girlfriend. I still have that picture today.

That same day, my dog was riddled with gunfire for barking at some German soldiers. My brothers saw it happen while working in the field next to the road. When the dog barked, the soldiers were ordered to stop and kill it. They were trained to kill men *or* dogs. It seemed to make no difference.

The Armenian's Warning

My next-to-youngest sister, Willie, was a good-hearted and intelligent girl. Just before the Battle of the Bridge, on September 16, she had gone to Arnhem to stay overnight at her boyfriend's farm. This young farmer's son was named Evert ten Bosch, Bart's cousin. He lived on the edge of Arnhem, so he and Willie must have watched the attack closely.

When Arnhem was evacuated, the ten Bosch men were allowed to stay with a few cows and pigs. Some German soldiers moved in with them, and were in charge of gathering livestock from across the river.

While I was visiting at the ten Bosch farm one afternoon in late November, 1944, the Germans were attempting to butcher a large, fat pig. They showed little skill, and I was afraid they might kill the pig without butchering it properly. Since food had become scarce and I didn't want the screaming, hollering animal to go to waste, I offered to help them. I said that I needed some bacon to bring back to my family. Soon, the large hog was nicely butchered and hanging on a ladder.

As I'd hoped, the Germans gave me a small package of meat for my help.

As I was preparing to leave in a steady downpour of rain, a cattle wagon stopped in front of the yard. I immediately recognized the driver: the crazy Armenian soldier I had encountered when last looking for Moebius.

The Armenian threw down the lines, jumped off the wagon seat, and headed straight toward me, hollering, "*Du komnst aus Angeren*!" You are from Angeren! He remembered me.

However, this time the soldier was much different. Stiff-like, but not as extreme, he shook my hand. Suddenly, I could not help feeling sorry for him, so far away from his homeland, Armenia.

When he said, "I am cold. Let's go inside," I agreed, following suit.

In I went, back into ten Bosch's house. Willie greeted me, confused and anxious when she saw who was with me. The Armenian plopped a basket full of stolen goods on the table, shaking his head like a dog and sending droplets of water from his soaked hair all over the kitchen.

"Your horses will get wet," I told him, eyeing the basket. "Do you want to leave them out there in the freezing cold?"

The Armenian waved a hand. "I have to go back there and bring more cattle anyway. Just leave them standing." Then, nodding at the basket, he said, "I found everything in there in Angeren and Huissen." He produced several bottles of schnapps wine, cigars, and jewelry. Poor Willie watched with wide eyes and bated breath, until the Armenian stopped suddenly, turning to me and asking out of the blue, "I say, what were you *really* doing in Angeren a few weeks ago?"

My whole body froze as he eyed me. Feigning calmness again, I answered steadily the same as I had before, that I'd been looking for bulls. I realized that I was in a serious situation. What did this hardened war veteran know? Other German soldiers were around us, and although they weren't paying much attention at the moment, I knew that if the Armenian's behavior turned fanatic like last time, I would not be able to calm him. Too many soldiers would have his back.

Fortunately, at that moment, another soldier brought him a plate of food, and the Armenian started wolfing his meat and bread down. I could tell that he demanded and drew authority. He was clearly the one in charge of this small operation, perhaps because he was the oldest.

While eating, he told me the cattle gathering was almost finished; only a few strays remained. Then he told me a story that chilled me right to the bone.

"Yesterday," he said, wiping his mouth on his sleeve, eyes trained on my face, "a red-nosed P-51 Mustang made an emergency landing on your very farm. Funny, huh? I took the American pilot prisoner. Here, somebody give me paper and pencil."

A soldier scrambled off, returning moments later with a piece of paper and pen. The Armenian started a rough sketch of my farm, then drew what looked like a crude version of a house. He pointed at the house. "This right here used to be the butcher's shop. I'm sure you knew that. We're using it as a local command post house now, and that's where I took the American to be interrogated."

I could feel him watching me closely, so I made sure not to twitch so much as a muscle in my face. "The American tried to escape," he said slowly. "So I told my soldiers to shoot him. Proud to say they didn't miss in the dark. Killed him. He's buried across the street from that butcher's house right now. Interesting story, isn't it?"

I knew the American pilot couldn't be Moebius, but from the way the Armenian's eyes were bearing into mine, the warning was all the same. *I know what you're doing*, those eyes said. *I'm watching you.*

The next spring, after the war, I found the grave of the shot pilot. I also reported the incident to authorities, and was present when the Americans identified him and reburied him elsewhere. Today, nearly 60 years later, I am still trying to locate his family to inform them of what and how the pilot died. So far, I have not found them.

Hitler Youths

Wim had a nice bicycle, but no signed papers to keep it with. One day, he came back home to Mr. and Mrs. Goedheer's on foot, saying that the Germans had stolen his bike.

"But I know where they stored it," he said, panting slightly. "The backyard of a villa. It's fenced and guarded by a soldier who walks around and around the building." He paused. "I need my bike, Gys."

I nodded. Bikes were virtually our only mode of transportation these days.

Together, we formed a plan. After observing the villa from a distance, we decided that I'd sneak inside the yard and toss the bike over the fence to Wim. We made a hand sign that Wim was supposed to make in case of any oncoming danger.

Everything went fine, and Wim rode away with his bike, thinking I was in the clear, too. But when I started climbing back over the fence, the guard saw me.

"Halt. Stop!" he hollered.

I launched myself up and over the fence. When I dropped to the ground, instant pain exploded in my foot. I had landed on a board with some nails, and a nail had gone through one of my shoes. As the guard started shooting, I freed myself, zigzagging away. I ran for my life, heading for the hospital from which I entered through the back door.

A nice, young nurse took off my shoe and saw all the blood. Smiling slightly, something I took as a good sign, she told me that I'd have to wait a while for the doctor, but my injury wasn't the most serious she'd seen all day.

Relief spread through me. We got to talking while I waited, and she informed me that the hospital had a serious food shortage. I said that if possible, I could help by bringing apples.

The doctor came, examined my foot, and told me to take it easy for a few days as the nurse busied herself with wrapping it. Approaching the subject of apples again, I said that if he could supply me and a few other men with Red Cross papers for a horse wagon, there was a good possibility I could help them. The doctor did so, thanking me.

A few days later, I asked Wim, Jan, and my Resistance friend Paul Roelofsen to join me on the hunt for apples. The four of us successfully reached Westervoort, only getting stopped once by German soldiers who, after seeing our Red Cross papers, let us continue. We picked apples undisturbed, working like beavers. No arrangements had been made for the hospital to pay us, but neither my brothers nor Paul mentioned that fact once. Perhaps we all knew that money had no value, or maybe in that critical period of life and death, human greatness rose to the surface. We all just tried to help and survive together.

When the wagons were full, we returned to the Yssel Bridge toward the hospital. But as we neared Duiyen by Velp, three young Hitler Youths, none older than 16, halted us.

The oldest and meanest of them marched up to my wagon, which was in front of the others, and ordered me to unload by the side of the road.

"No," I said.

The boy looked as if he had been struck, his face turning scarlet. I pulled out my Red Cross papers to show him that I was allowed to travel, but the boy didn't even glance down. He was trembling with rage. As soon as his young cronies came flanking up behind him, he pointed his gun at me.

"See that farm next to the road?" he said, teeth gritted, shaking. "Go to the barnyard. Now."

With a bullet just seconds away from entering my brain, I had no choice. I was pushed and prodded by two of the boys into the barn, where the oldest demanded I stand against the wall with my hands held high. Wim, Jan, and Paul watched from a great distance while the remaining Hitler Youth started unloading our apples, throwing them out onto the road by the armful. He and his friends wanted the horses and wagons, I suspected, to go to Arnhem and steal goods and furniture.

Meanwhile, the oldest Hitler Youth started kicking me and poking his rifle so hard into my ribs that days later, blue circles would blossom underneath my skin and remain for several weeks.

While they were unloading the apples and hurting me, a Volkswagen passing on the road slowed way down, then backed up. Whoever was inside drove to the barnyard and stopped. Two officers in neat uniforms stepped out, asking what was going on. The Youths jumped to attention like puppets.

"My friends and I were just getting apples for Red Cross," I explained, "when these three boys – the other one is over by my wagons – stopped us and threatened me." One of the officers raised an eyebrow, so I once again took out my papers and showed it to him. His expression softened. He rounded on the Hitler Youths.

"You should feel ashamed of yourselves!"

The Youths received a dressing down and were told to disappear at once. I watched them go, no more than children running off into the darkness. The officers walked me back to my wagon where they each picked up an apple on the ground, saluted us, and left.

When all was quiet, I caught my companions' eyes and nodded toward the barn.

"One of the boys forgot his rifle," I said. Jan and I looked at each other, walked over, and took the gun. I placed it snugly between two apple boxes, hidden from view. Jan shook his head, smiling. I still have this rifle as a souvenir today.

When we unloaded the apples at the hospital (we'd picked up as many as we could off the ground) the head doctor and the same nurse who'd looked at my foot came out and personally thanked us all.

The Russian Girl

A few days later, we heard that Paul Roelofsen had been arrested by the Gestapo. The Nazi police had simply shown up at his house and accused him of being a member of the Resistance, arresting him on the spot. His older brother, a well-respected and strong Resistance member named Roelof, told my brothers and me that he was locked up in a villa cellar in Velp.

I immediately went with Roelof to investigate. From a distance, as evening gathered darkness, we heard Paul screaming in agony as he was being tortured. It sounded terrifying. When I glanced sideways at Roelof, his eyes were squeezed shut in pain.

Both Paul and Roelof were big, strong men, daring and dependable. I had often wondered if they were *too* aggressive, but at the same time, I knew that several members of their old Resistance group had been killed in cold blood by the Germans. Their grief had eventually turned them both into fighters.

I knew Paul had no chance of surviving in the cellar, no matter how strong he was. He was being exposed to the worst type of torture. Experts at tormenting would try to get as much information out of him as they could, then kill him when he had nothing left. Roelof and I made plans to attack the guards around the villa as soon as possible.

Suddenly, I remembered Paul's wife, who was late in her third pregnancy, and their two children. I told Roelof that they should be taken to safety at once. Paul would not break down easily, but the Germans often kidnapped relatives and threatened them – or worse – in order to coerce prisoners into talking.

Roelof informed me of a place in the woods near Dieren where there was a secret barrack owned by some of his friends. That same night, I picked up Paul's wife and kids and took them on bicycles to the barrack, following Roelof's instructions. We arrived there in the dark, Paul's wife completely exhausted and her kids scared.

Greeting us at the door, a Russian lady about twenty-five years old lit a candle and helped us inside. She gave Paul's wife the only bed left and gave the kids some blankets, explaining to me in a whisper that the hiding place belonged to a Resistance group with an underground tunnel used for escape.

The Russian girl's name was Natjana. She was striking, with a dark complexion and coal-black eyes. She told me she had been taken prisoner in 1942 and transported to Germany for slave labor like millions of others. Those unfortunate Russians always performed slave labor in the most dangerous places, like factories or mines. With the help of a young Dutchman, Natjana had escaped as a stowaway on a Rhine riverboat headed downstream to Holland. Somehow, she had gotten tangled up in Resistance activities and had decided to join. By the way she spoke and her strong personality, I knew she was one of the barrack's leaders.

Since it was well past midnight, I spent the night there. For a few hours, we stayed awake, and Natjana displayed other talents by playing the guitar and singing Russian songs with a beautiful alto voice. It was a welcoming break from our tense and dangerous existence. I could not help but take an immediate liking to her, even more so after she told me some fascinatingly sad stories.

"My family," she whispered once, "I don't know if they're alive or not. I haven't heard from them for several years... I just wonder what I'll find when I return home."

She cried afterward. I held her and tried to console her, telling her that it would not be long before she was back in Russia. Wiping at the tears on her cheeks, she told me that I was very brave for bringing someone else's wife and children to safety.

"Thank you," I said. And, after a moment – "What ever became of the Dutchman who helped you escape?"

"He's still in Germany, helping other people escape camps," Natjana said sadly. "I think – I think I'll wait for him before returning to Russia."

During the night, a soft knocking on the barrack door awakened us. I was lying on the floor close to the door, but I didn't attempt to open it since I was only a guest. One of the barrack's leaders guided two other men inside, helping a wounded third. This wounded man was an American pilot from a B-17 shot down the day before. I was glad when Natjana and the men in charge immediately starting taking care of this wounded American. He was half-unconscious and seemed to be in bad shape. The men told me they had walked quite a distance in the dark to get away from the crash site and out of the immediate area.

The American was in good hands and resting when I left Natjana the next morning. I told her and the others that I would try to stop by again if I ever could. Then saying goodbye to Paul's family and assuring his wife I would do everything in my power to save her husband, I rode my bicycle back to Velp.

When I found Roelof, he outlined our plan in detail, saying there were five men willing to participate in the job. Then he reached into his coat pocket, smiling, and produced the smallest silver pistol I had ever seen, handing it out to me.

I stared at that lady's pistol in amazement, thinking about the possibility of using it against modern automatic killing devices. However, I took it anyway. I knew that Paul was being exposed to the worst treatment and something had to be done quickly; there was no time for me to complain about the size of my pistol.

"Do you think anyone could have betrayed your brother?" I asked Roelof the day before our planned rescue mission. "The Gestapo must have been tipped off about his Resistance work, don't you think?"

"I have no clue," Roelof said.

But as we sat there, I remembered one evening several weeks prior where I had arrived at Paul's place to pick up an old Jewish couple to deliver them to safety. When I entered the farm on the backside – a habit I had formed as a precaution – I'd bumped into a young Dutch girl and a German soldier making love behind the door.

I had seen the girl before. She worked for Paul in the house and on the farm. Also, I knew that German military men were around Paul's quite often, since Paul was the local head of the food supply. He dealt with them for distribution and protecting food from theft. Therefore, it wasn't that strange that the girl and German should end up together.

So I'd let it go. But thinking back now, that particular girl, who worked dutifully for Paul, witnessed many things, including Resistance work. She knew, of course, that I had taken the Jewish couple and the families to safe places.

I relayed this to Roelof. He started.

"Damnit," he murmured. "That girl *did* disappear right after Paul's arrest."

We agreed that the girl was most likely the problem. She could have easily been planted at Paul's by the Gestapo. There were spies everywhere. Usually Dutch girls like her were paid very well for their service and rewarded with all kinds of favors, especially food. When people became hungry, they became desperate. It was a sad, but real truth.

The next morning, after thinking things over, I decided to wrap the small silver pistol in an oil cloth and bury it under the railroad in a certain spot where we housed. Instead, I would use a sharp bayonet I had taken from the Germans while in Angeren. I thought it more ideal because it was quiet and certainly had better penetration.

But that night, when the five of us men met that evening, Roelof made an announcement – Paul had escaped!

Our tense feelings immediately relaxed, for the plan would have been extremely dangerous to undertake.

Roelof told us what happened. During the week Paul was held captive, he had seized a chance to hide a good, heavy spoon. When his guard was on the other side of the villa, Paul would sharpen the spoon on the cement floor in the shape of a screwdriver. It took him several days to make the spoon sharp enough, and several days after *that* to loosen the screws in the small cellar window.

With his enormous strength, Paul had lifted the window out and pulled himself to freedom. In the dark, he'd walked to Roelof's farm, where he obtained nun clothes the Resistance had on hand for disguises. He then escaped on a bicycle across the river by ferry, to his brother-in-law's house in Brummen. He had lost almost thirty pounds in one week.

I didn't see Paul again until after the war, when he told me the whole story in detail and showed me the spoon. He also showed me his shirt – or what was left of it. It had been cut loose from his back since the cloth had grown into his flesh. This was a result of the terrible beatings he had endured.

After hearing of Paul's escape, I went back home, relieved and happy. But happiness was only short-lived in the presence of war, shattered at the merest touch. Paul's family, his wife with a newborn baby in her arms, came back to Velp in the nick of time. They brought devastating news with them.

Almost everyone back in the barrack had been caught and murdered by the Germans. Including Natjana.

Escape to the North

It turned out that the Dutch girl didn't just betray Paul. Soon, I heard that the Gestapo was looking for me, too. Roelof, my brothers, and I decided I should hide out for a while, so the very next day I said goodbye to my family again. I left for Apeldoorn early in the morning, never before realizing how weird it was to be such an outcast and fugitive. I wondered what awaited me while bicycling away from my loved ones toward a strange country.

After I picked up some papers in Apeldoorn, I headed north on a lonely stretch of highway toward Zwolle. The temperature was clear below zero, and even though my legs continued pedaling and I was dressed in many layers, I was miserable. The traffic was light, perhaps because of the bitter cold.

Once, a Volkswagen passed me. I stared at it as it passed, because for some reason, the sight of it gave me chills, as if I had seen the vehicle before.

No more than a minute later, two English spitfires from the sky dived and fired at it. I screeched to a stop, waiting with my breath fogging the air for something more to happen. But nothing did. The planes disappeared, leaving the vehicle in front of me on fire and riddled with holes.

I drew close to the flames. Heat bloomed out at me. Two German officers and the driver were dead, bleeding and burning. It had all happened in just a few seconds. Just a couple short bursts from the planes' 50 caliber machine guns, and those lives were gone.

As I stood gaping at the bodies, my memory was again stirred. And suddenly I realized the reason why. I was almost positive that the two dead German officers were the same ones who had rescued me from the Hitler Youths and each taken an apple before saluting goodbye.

I quickly retreated from the scene, shaking.

When I reached the Zwolle Bridge over the Yssel River, all kinds of people, mostly women from big cities, were headed north in search of food. Young men were in hiding everywhere, afraid of being sent to slave labor camps. Several times I witnessed people collapsing by the roadside, dying of starvation or exhaustion, but I did not have any food to give them.

****

The Resistance had planned for me to report to Leewarden as a seed potato buyer. I took another long, hard day of bicycling until I reached the area, hungry and tired. When I passed through Zwolle, a city of more than 100,000 people, I saw places with long soup lines where hungry people ate for free. I did not mind the wait, but when the ladler gave me a small bowl of thin, watery soup, I was dismayed. While sipping the meek broth, it started to snow; snowflakes landed in my bowl and melted slowly. I knew I had to look for shelter.

I stopped beside an old, weathered schoolhouse and examined the inside. The floors were covered with straw for hundreds of people, mostly from western cities. Most people were sitting or trying to secure spots to sleep. Many of them were scratching at their heads like animals, for lice and fleas had become huge problems. I decided to continue onward into a better part of Zwolle.

When I pedaled through a neighborhood of large homes, I spotted a sign on one that read:

NIKS

Dentist. In these times, *dentist* also meant someone who would take care of more than teeth if a man or woman appeared on his doorstep with a bullet wound. I was guessing that the dentist received many customers, and was used to letting people inside. Resolving to try my luck, I stopped and rang the doorbell. A girl in a white apron opened the door about six inches.

"Hello?" she asked, peering suspiciously over my shoulder as if expecting a Nazi to be crouching right behind me.

"Hi." My whole body was shivering uncontrollably now. "Could I speak to the doctor?"

The girl didn't answer; instead, she looked me up and down and asked, "Are you hurting bad?"

"I need food and shelter," I said. My lips were so numb I could barely speak. "Everywhere else is full."

For a moment, I thought the girl would shut the door in my face. But after a few seconds of hesitant consideration, she disappeared and returned with the dentist, whose forehead creased in worry at my appearance.

"I've already fed seventeen people today, and some are sleeping on my floor as we speak," he said, not hostile, but frowning all the same.

"P-please." My chattering teeth made me stutter. When the doctor only looked at me, I drew my coat tighter around me and turned around. Maybe the house next door would –

"Wait."

I turned to face the dentist again. He sighed, opening his door wider. "Come on in. Hurry, before the cold gets in, too."

Gratefully, I followed the dentist into a warm, cluttered kitchen. Just as he'd said, many people, from a fidgety, twelve-year-old boy to a rail-like old man were clustered around the table or lying on rugs on the floor, talking or sleeping. After eating a hot meal, I slept deeply on a blanket near the oven.

I said goodbye to the dentist the next morning while heading for Leevwarden, but I told him I'd be back someday to thank him. After the war, I stopped at his house twice to deliver boxes of apples from our orchard trees, and some 52 years later I called asking if the dentist was still alive. Unfortunately, he had passed away, but his son remembered the story and is now a dentist too.

****

Only one other event worth mentioning happened before I reached Leevwarden. In the sky, hundreds of four-engine bombers were flying toward Germany. The Americans were doing their duty. I was suddenly struck with the realization that while I was only 100 miles from home, those brave men were thousands of miles away from their homes and flying further away still.

While I parked on the road to watch and admire the planes with their small vapor trails, I saw one get hit by German artillery and descend in flames. No parachutes opened up. Ten young men suffered the ultimate, adding to a long list of casualties that could never be erased.

I waited until the big plane plunged to the earth before resuming my escape north.

Capture and Escape

In Leevwarden, I acted as a potato buyer for a month with success. I liked it there. It was peaceful and quiet, far away from any destructive activities, so that I could almost imagine at times that the war was only a nightmare I had recently awakened from. The man and his wife whom I stayed with had no children, and the food was good. The only mention of the catastrophe still raging worldwide was the secret radio messages we listened to from England every night. Each time the radio announcer spoke in the Allies' favor, we cheered and applauded, clapping each other on the back. Each time Hitler made a gain, we stared somberly into the fire, not saying a word.

In the first part of December, 1944, U.S. General George Patton galloped across France with his feared Third Army, until even an express line of thousands of trucks could not get supplies to his troops fast enough. This prompted the General to say, "We go on till our tanks run dry and then walk to defeat the Hun!" In reality, I think, the idea was nothing more than a release of steam for this iron-eating flamboyant old warrior.

In addition to all the General Patton's good qualities, I believe he possessed a sixth sense that allowed him to suspect when he would be counterattacked. Patton's intuition became a reality when the Germans launched an attack toward the Ardennes Mountains – sometimes called the Battle of the Bulge – on December 16, 1944.

They attacked with crack troops and hundreds of new tanks, making enormous gains over the next few days. It was bitterly cold with heavy snow: the coldest winter in 38 years. All of these factors created a scare amongst the Allied high command. Although few said so, many felt, including Eisenhower, that the war could still be lost.

Almost every time the skies cleared overhead planes would be dropping bombs only minutes later. I was so worried about my family that one day I decided to return to Velp, no matter the costs. The couple I'd been staying with advised me to take another route rather than the bridge near Zwolle, for it was rumored that heavy patrols were guarding that river now. Instead, I took a country route and crossed another, smaller river closer to Velp.

On this return trip, I was stopped toward evening near Gorzel, a launching place for the new German weapons: the V-1 flying bombs! They were no secret weapons, but still hellish machines that made terrifying sounds. In German, V-1 actually stood for *Vergeltungs Waffe* number 1, translated in English: Revenge Weapon number 1. These bombs were unreliable and fell everywhere they were not supposed to. When they flew overhead, everything, from the ground to the very tips of our fingertips, vibrated. As long as we heard that vibration, we sighed with relief... but if the noise ever stopped overhead, *everyone* stopped in terror.

One of these V-1's had crashed to the road shortly after takeoff. As I approached the explosion site, I saw several civilians already arrested and working at gunpoint, shoveling dirt to fill up the crater the bomb had created. As soon as I saw this, I tried to turn around, but a German saw me and shouted, "Halt!"

With a gun trained on my head, I was forced to pile my bicycle in a heap nearby and join the other civilians in their toil. Traffic was stopped and all able men put to work. Nobody paid attention to the permits I tried to bring out. The soldiers only acted frenzied and aggressive, barking out orders.

We worked until dark. Only some of the older men were released. The Germans lined the rest of us up and marched us into a barn nearby. Most of my fellow prisoners were mere skeletons and moved about in a daze. I knew that nothing good was planned for us – if they were keeping us tonight, they would not release us tomorrow.

With only a little daylight left, I spotted a roof window in the barn before being herded into the building with about fifteen other men. The doors were bolted behind us, so we had to feel around inside the place until someone lighted some matches they had in their pockets. A few men tried to rest in a pile of straw, tired after a long day of shoveling with no food. We were all anxious about our fate.

I spoke to a young man I had befriended during the shoveling. "What do you think about trying to escape?" I asked quietly.

The fellow's eyes lit up in the low light of the flames. "I think that's a hell of a good idea. You got a plan?"

Nodding up in the direction of the barn's window, I said, "I'll show you if you give me a lift."

My new friend smirked. "Deal." He helped me clamber up onto the barn's rafters. Once up on the wide, wooden beams, I pulled him up as well and we made our vigilant way toward the roof window, our only hope. We opened the window with bated breaths, as everyone below us looked up in awe. I threw my long, leather overcoat onto the roof. Then, wiggling through the window with my young friend pushing, I squeezed out, pulling him out with me. It helped that the war had made us both skinny.

After crouching on the roof for a while, we did not notice any guards, so we slid down and headed for the pile of bicycles. My handlebars were twisted. As I tried straightening them, but my friend hastily took off on his own, making noise on the frozen ground.

"STOP!" An alerted guard stormed after him, hollering, rife ready. When his target became too far away, he got into position, pointed his rifle carefully in the direction of my friend, placed his finger on the trigger…

The guard did not see me. I took my chance, throwing my bike at his back. He staggered to the ground, his rifle flying. When the rifle landed, I sprinted to it and grabbed it, turning it on the guard, who was bellowing like a bull.

"Quiet," I warned. The guard ceased yelling immediately. I started backing away toward the barn. When I reached it, I un-bolted the door. Before sticking around to see what became of that, I returned to the guard once more, grabbed my bike from his feet as one would tread around a serpent, and started pedaling away as fast as I could. When I was about a mile away, because I couldn't bicycle well with the gun in one hand, I chucked the rifle far away from me, hopefully in a tangle of bushes where nobody would find it until after the war.

I bicycled all the way back home, never stopping once.

The Hunt

Finally making it back to Velp, I was troubled to find my mother in worsening condition. Although Mr. and Mrs. Goedheer were some of the best hosts in town, even they could not provide her with enough food to keep her healthy. Her eyes had a sunken, sickly look and her skin was thin and pale. She was happy to see me, smiling when I walked in the door, but I had to embrace her carefully. Even her shoulders now felt fragile and weak.

Out of earshot, Wim and I discussed the food situation in the kitchen, trying to come up with ways we could either acquire good food or hunt for some ourselves. Wim folded his arms, leaning against a door frame.

"Some steers have been running loose across the Yssel River," he said.

I thought about that. While loading apples in Bart's orchard a few months before, I had seen two year-old Holstein steers in good shape, although extremely wild.

After some deliberation, I nodded. "I think it's the best chance we've got," I agreed. "There's no other way we can obtain good meat."

"Let's go see Bart and ask what he thinks," Wim said. "He lives across the Yssel, so he'd know all about the steer."

However, when we visited Bart that night, he shook his head. "Too risky. There's no way you could actually catch one, let alone kill it. And how would you transport all that weight across the river even if you *did* manage to shoot one down? You'd get shot by a German before you could make it halfway."

Wim and I looked at each other, the same frustration reflected in each other's eyes.

"I'm tired of going without food," Wim said firmly. "And I'm *sick* of my mother looking like a ghost. Something has to be done."

We left Bart massaging his head, calling after us in a weak voice, "You'll never catch one unless you use a gun!"

On a dark and rainy night near the end of January, 1945, we crossed the Yssel in a borrowed rowboat, getting off at a point just before the river dumped into the Rhine. The Yssel was not a wide river, necessarily, but dangerously swift where we crossed. The rough weather was not in our favor, so we slept in a barn of Bart's that was only a little ways from his farmhouse. That whole night, we saw no one.

The following morning, the rainfall had stopped, leaving everything glistening and wet. Wim and I went to work lifting several gates off their hinges and lining them into a chute, with the narrowest end leading into the barn and the widest in the direction of the wild steer. We hoped to drive the mighty animals into the barn by chasing them toward the chute's opening.

All at once, rifle shots rang loud and clear on a neighbor's farm. Wim and I made our way cautiously toward this farm to see what was happening, for we knew the Dutch owner, a bachelor named van Zadelfhof who had often helped us retrieve apples.

"Who knows?" whispered Wim. "Maybe he'll help us chase down the oxen."

As we drew close, we saw a group of lively Germans practicing shooting cans and bottles in van Zadelfhof's front yard. The Germans hardly glanced at us when we asked where van Zadelfhof was.

"Not here," one replied, closing an eye and taking another shot with a *bang*!

Wim and I stood watching them shoot for a few minutes. It started drizzling again. Just as the sun came out, giving a nice break between showers, one of the soldiers asked if we would like to try a few shots just for fun. He elbowed his buddies after he said this, and they all laughed. Silly, peaceful Dutchmen can't shoot, they were probably thinking.

I caught Wim's eye.

"Go ahead," he told me. "Try."

One, last glass milk bottle stood on the fence post as a target. I walked to the bottle and laid it down so that the small, circular opening faced us instead. The Germans watched and smirked. I took the rifle from the soldier, positioned myself as they snickered to one another, and pulled the trigger.

Bang! *Crack*! The bullet went right through the opening of the milk bottle and shot the bottom out perfectly.

The soldiers stopped grinning, suddenly tense and serious. I stood up, handing back the rifle without a word.

Silence. Now Wim and I had the complete attention of the German soldiers, the two of us facing and staring down the five or so of them. Finally, the same soldier who'd offered me his rifle cleared his throat and said gruffly, "What're you guys doing here? This is no-man's land."

Ready to drop at a single twitch of their rifles, I said, "We're trying to catch a steer. Food's getting scarce and any steers on this land belong to my brother-in-law, so it's rightfully ours if we can catch one."

The Germans looked at each other in an uncomfortable moment of stillness. Then, the soldier with the rifle cleared his throat again and asked, "Want some help with that?"

Perhaps my shooting had demanded their respect or perhaps the soldiers were bored. For whatever reason, though, two more of them unexpectedly offered to help, too. As the soldiers walked ahead of us, loading their rifles, I told Wim in our own language, "This looks like it'll be quite the hunt, doesn't it?"

The soldier with the loaded rifle must have heard me. Looking back, he said in perfect Dutch: "We might lose this war, but I love to shoot."

Surprised that he knew Dutch, I told him that we wanted to catch a steer alive, so that we could swim it across the river. No shooting. The German laughed.

When we found the steers, they ran away, since they had been chased and shot at so many times. But with a little herding skill and a trace of luck, the Germans, Wim, and I chased one into our chute and in the barn. Once the steer was trapped, we shut the doors, locking ourselves inside with the running, bucking animal.

The fun was just beginning, though. Still needing to halter it, Wim and I mimicked cowboys we had seen on Wild West shows before the war, twirling long ropes and trying to wrap it around the steer's neck. The Germans roared with laughter as they watched. One shouted that he'd never seen such an entertaining show. Meanwhile, the beast ran and snorted, sometimes coming right after Wim or me with his big horns ready to attack. We took turns leading and chasing.

Finally, with some more luck, we wrestled the steer down and put a halter on him. His big belly rose up and down furiously, the air entering and exiting his nose in big huffs. As we left, now leading the steer, we thanked the Germans for their help. They stood watching us disappear toward the river, wiping the tears from their eyes and waving goodbye.

****

It started raining again. Soon, Wim and I were soaked to the skin, and the worst was yet to come – crossing the river.

It took more than two hours to reach the Yssel with the steer, who resisted our every move. When we finally, finally came to our little boat, we had to rest. I looked at our prize – or was he our doom? The brute stood there, as worn-out as we were with his tongue hanging out and the rain skidding off his coat. I suddenly realized how extremely dangerous the crossing would be, but neither Wim or I talked about it – we just sat there for a while in the pouring rain, getting ready for the final home run.

In desperation, I believe a person possesses extra strength and determination to survive. The steer wrestling would have been impossible in normal times, as would have the crossing of the river. I still do not know how we managed it.

Ultimately, we couldn't ignore the ferocity of the pounding downpour any longer. I clambered into the boat, taking a deep breath, and started rowing. Wim held the rope, as well as a long stick in order to keep the steer's front legs from hitting the boat. The steer himself had no choice but to plunge into the ice-cold water and start swimming after us. As bucketfuls of pouring rain fell upon us, we bent our heads forward, urging the beast onward, the current's violent tug matched up against the strength of my arms as they rowed.

Halfway across, the steer rolled over in the water and went under. Wim screamed, "Row, Gys! Row faster! He's drowning!"

Then the steer resurfaced, blowing water like a whale.

I could not see. I did not know what was backward or what was forward. I could only tell myself to keep going, keep going, or we would all drown in the torrent of water lashing at us from every direction.

When we finally reached the other side, my arms were weak and limp. I dropped the oars and sank onto the ground.

Thank you, God, I thought.

Wim fell down beside me, slinging his arm around my shoulder and panting. The steer scrambled onto the bank after us, huffing, snorting out water.

"We did it," I breathed. "Wim, we made it across!" It was one of the greatest victories of our lives.

Just as the rain started to lighten, a civilian controller dressed in a long, leather overcoat strode toward us. His boots splashed in the mud. Wim and I looked up at him, our own knees still on the ground.

"What are you doing with that steer?" the controller shouted. "It is against the law to move an animal without a permit!" He started puffing out his chest, running his mouth more.

But I was tired: not just from crossing the Yssel, but tired of watching people get murdered, of witnessing innocent people get shot, of all the unfairness. I was tired of men like the controller ordering everyone around.

So before the controller could say anything more, I stopped him. "Go to hell, why don't you?"

And standing up with renewed strength, Wim and I gathered our steer and left the controller gaping after us, standing in the easing rain.

Liberation, At Last

After butchering the steer and packaging the meat, my family grew stronger. Color reappeared in my mother's cheeks. I was at peace knowing that the war wouldn't starve us. Mother and Father, Willie and Jane – none of them would die of an empty stomach.

Meanwhile, our secret radio gave news of a Yalta Conference that would determine the end of the war. We could feel it all drawing to a close. Soon, a friendly rumbling from Allied tanks could be heard from the other side of the river. There was excitement in the air, an unexplainable feeling. The Germans themselves transformed from hostile, shouting, and cocky dictators to nervous wrecks. They compensated by being twice as loud, twice as aggressive. Jan spotted a whole row of German pontoon bridge material loaded on camouflaged wagons with a guard on watch. They were parked under trees close to where we housed, scurrying this way and that like flustered ants.

These soldiers would fire a gun a few times and then relocate to fire the same gun again in a different place. This gave the impression to any

Allied observers that the Germans possessed more pieces of artillery than they actually had.

When Roelof called together a Resistance meeting that evening, he asked for volunteers to cross the Rhine River to inform the Allies to cease firing. For several days, we had heard the noise of Allied heavy equipment being moved for attack across the river. The long-awaited liberation was in the making, but heavy, unnecessary damage was being done to Velp.

"The Allies don't know that the Germans are basically done for," Roelof said. "They don't need to bomb us any more in order to win."

Along with me, a one-armed ex-marine from Rotterdam volunteered to relay this message to the Allies. He had lost his arm in the Moerdyk battle and was a brave Resistance member.

But that night, just as we neared the water's edge where a rowboat was placed, a terrible barrage of what seemed like a thousand cannons burst loose. It was the beginning of the attack. We were too late to stop it.

The one-armed marine and I dove into a nearby ditch. While lying flat on my stomach, a grenade exploded close to me. I was knocked unconscious for a long time. When I awoke, I was completely covered with dirt debris, and the one-armed marine was gone. I never saw him again.

Dizzy, I crawled out of the ditch unscathed. It was now nearing the early morning hours. As bombs shook the ground beneath my feet and exploded with a cacophony of sounds, I returned to Velp, ducking and diving whenever I heard gunshots.

When I knocked on the door and my mother greeted me, her face turned bloodless. "Is that you, Gys?" she asked, hushed.

I nodded.

"Mark this day, Mom," I said. April 16, 1945. "Today we're getting rescued."

As if in effect, only a few hours after my mother had successfully finished cleaning me free of dirt and debris, the artillery barrage ceased, followed by silence. The stillness slunk into every household of Velp, holding its breath, waiting, hoping…

Then, with no resistance, the American troops appeared on the other side of the Rhine, crossing it by the thousands – our liberators. As my family and I stood watching them drive out the last of the Germans, I was emotionally overcome. Mother put her face into my father's chest and cried.

The whole town of Velp began vibrating from hundreds of monstrous tanks that moved by. The first ones were equipped with mine feelers, steel balls the size of soccer balls attached with chains that rolled over the ground. Thousands of troops riding motorized vehicles, jeeps, motorcycles, and artillery pieces followed the tanks. Only a few walked on foot. They rumbled past with a noise and excitement that filled every person watching.

The population went wild, waving flags, girls climbing up on vehicles as they chugged along. American soldiers shouted a few words to the crowds lining the streets – most didn't know what they were saying, but cheered anyhow. Some of the friendliest soldiers tossed out candy and cigarettes that the people in Velp caught with thrilled vigor. Seeing their special uniforms, I was reminded of Moebius, and wondered where he was at now, or if he were still alive.

Day and night, they kept coming, all headed for Germany. The American trucks, decorated with the white five-pointed star enclosed in a white circle, were loaded with food. Food distribution quarters were set up so that people could obtain good meals again. The terrible feeling and scare of hunger and starvation was over.

After five years of war, it was like a dream come true! The rightful world, so precious and so dear, had been regained, and I felt nothing less than the highest degree of admiration and gratefulness to our liberators – and to God – for being alive.

But though WWII officially ended in May of 1945, the repercussions of the war did not. People were still sick. Homes were still destroyed. Friends had still died, gotten shot, been tortured... I had no inkling whether the American pilot had survived or not, although Moebius *would* have a future impact on my life. I just didn't know it at the time. Nothing was certain.

We had a long road stretching ahead of us.

The Only Survivor

After several weeks of repairing and rebuilding what had been destroyed in Velp, my family talked about the possibility of returning to our farm on the other side of the river. What was waiting for us there? Nobody knew. We had heard wild stories from soldiers who had participated in the spring offensive about what Angeren now looked like, but we didn't know whether to believe the grim details or not.

I decided to go back alone and report to everyone what I saw. My mother made me a sandwich for the journey, which I fit into my pocket. My father told me to be safe. I received a permit from the liberators so that I could return to my old town. The office personnel who issued it to me pointed out all the dangers marked again and again on the map, showing where the minefields were. It struck me how concerned and helpful these new friends were. What a difference, and relief! The personnel asked me to report to them that night or in the morning after the inspection tour. Just in case I didn't, she wrote down my farm's address.

Upon reaching the pontoon bridge across the Rhine River, two American MP's stopped me and looked at my permit. Again, they warned me of possible danger and said that I should take extra caution and remain on the road. When one of them hollered after me to watch for booby traps, I had to turn around to ask him to explain. I had never heard of booby traps before.

It was a beautiful morning, May 15, 1945. However, Angeren itself contrasted greatly to the sunshine. In my mind, I had already prepared myself for a letdown, but with so much death and destruction everywhere around me, the disappointment ran much deeper, hitting me like a stone.

The stench of decaying cattle and horses lying around by the hundreds was sickening. I also spotted human bodies, just lying here and there. Unused ammunition littered the riddled ground. A German Tiger Tank lay upside-down in a ditch: sixty tons of steel tightly lodged. Heavy broken cable lay nearby as silent witnesses of a past attempt to upright it. Later, I heard a story that the tank still held some crew inside like a steel grave.

Twice on my way to the farm, I met Canadian cleanup crews who checked my permit. Both times, they cautioned me with sad smiles. I thanked them, admiring them as much as the Americans. They were performing gruesome tasks, having to douse dead cattle with gasoline to burn it. They also marked mine fields with white strips of lint and marked burned, broken-down vehicles.

Other than the cleanup crew, I saw nobody. Here and there, a stray and scared rabbit, cat, or dog moved about. It gave me a weird feeling, to be amidst such a quiet and depressing place. Even on this nice, bright day in May, all felt cold and lifeless.

****

Only when I was about a mile from my farm someone come near: a young, dirty-looking German soldier was riding his bike toward me.

He was an awful sight. Although he was wrapped in a thick, fur-lined coat, the coat hung loosely on him. He had a thin beard and was shaking as if cold or frightened. He raised his hands before I could even speak.

"I surrender, I surrender," the soldier said, voice trembling.

"Okay. It's alright." I put out my hands as if to console a startled, wild animal. "I won't hurt you. But don't surrender to me, surrender to the cleanup crew."

The soldier looked confused. Gazing around, he asked, "Is it over?"

"Yes. Didn't you know?"

For a second, the soldier just stared at me as if not daring to comprehend. Pressing his face into his hands, he started to cry – with joy, I soon realized. The soldier told me he had deserted the German army and had been hiding in a cellar. Once in a while, he'd shot a rabbit and found preserved food to sustain himself. It had barely kept him alive… he was little more than skin and bones. Only his fur-lined coat, which had come from Russia, had helped him survive the last Holland winter.

When asking me where the Canadian cleanup crew was, I pointed in the direction I had been coming from. "But," I said, "you might not want to approach them with that weapon."

Promptly, the soldier handed me his rifle. Then, he shrugged off his coat and placed it at my feet. "Have it," he said. "Please."

He was about to leave. But as I stood there with his coat and rifle, not quite knowing what to say, I could not stop looking at how skinny the boy was. An idea striking me, I reached into my pocket and brought out the sandwich my mother had made for me. The soldier took it in awe. He devoured it within a few bites.

"Thank you," he said. Then I watched as the young survivor peddled away, crying once more and waving goodbye. He was so frail and young, just a kid who, like me, was fortunate to be alive rather than returned to dust. Later that day, I handed his rifle to the Canadians.

After that strange episode, I finally made my way to my old home. After eight months, only the sturdiest of brick cellars on the farm were left intact. Peering down into the largest cellar floor, I saw the marks from an exploded hand grenade; apparently, some fighting had taken place there. Looking around, I soon found a grave and cross of a German soldier nearby. On the cross was written his name: *soldaat Klingenburg*. The dirt on the grave was still fresh.

The only survivor on our farm was a cat, which came peeking out from under a pile of half-burnt wood. I vaguely remembered the cat as one

Willie had fed and cared for many years before. *I'll have to tell her it's still alive*, I thought. Willie would like that.

I found our hidden radio untouched, still hidden in the cement water trough. I was happy to see it, because all through the awful war, it had seemed like a friend to us.

After looking around some more, Willie's cat meowed. It came nearer to me. Unbelievably, it acted as if it knew me after all this time.

I picked it up and held it, something I had never done before the war. But this time, as the cat started purring and digging her claws into my arm in a pleased gesture, it meant the world to me to hold a living animal in the middle of all the death and ruin. And I knew, then, that I would do everything in my power to make sure that another war never occurred again.

Life was too precious, too fragile, for humans to turn on each other. We needed to quit fighting, and start helping each other and learning from one another. It was the only way to never repeat our mistakes. The battle worth fighting for was not the war we humans had put ourselves in, but the battle of always being good, always learning from past faults, and to never, *ever* forget. No matter what.

"Come, fellows, the world needs mending," I whispered to the cat. She responded with another meow, the air moving in and out of her little nostrils, the life making her heart beat against her ribcage. I felt that pulse against my own chest like the life of hope, as I recalled the poem I had written on the school's blackboards so long ago. "Much can be done by everyone," I said into the open air, the cat purring. "Rewards for all who do."

Howard Moebius

Valley of the Shadow

"Yeah though I walk through the valley of the shadow of death, I will fear no evil for Thou art with me."

A brief story of a visit to Holland during World War II

by Howard E. Moebius

First Lieutenant U. S. Army Air corps

Single Engine Pilot

357th Fighter Group

364th Squadron

8th Air force

Stationed at Leiston, England

Relating to events from September 19, 1944 to February 12, 1945

©1993, 2014

To my dear friends in Holland —

You risked your lives to hide me from the Germans. You fed me and nursed me back to health. You found a way for me to escape back into Allied held territory.

For this —

I express my everlasting gratitude.

To Chuck Yeager —

Little did you know that when you related your experience of bailing out over enemy held territory that those very words would save the life of one of your listeners.

For this, I say —

Thanks Chuck – It was the right stuff.

This is a story that I recorded in 1957 when I could still recall much that had happened during my last six months in Europe from the fall of 1944 until the beginning of March 1945. I had graduated from flight school in January of 1944 in Eagle Pass, Texas as a Second Lieutenant in the Class of 44A. This was an Advanced Single Engine Army Air Corps Base where I had trained in North American AT 6s. The last two weeks, I flew P40s since P51s were not available for Advance Training at that time. We were required to get at least 20 hours of transitional fighter training. P40s were being phased out of combat and replaced by P47s, P38s and P51s. I also had had additional P40 time at Pinellas Airfield in St. Petersburg, Florida prior to being shipped overseas.

We sailed to England in an unescorted round bottom troop ship that went just slightly faster than the German U boats that were constantly being picked up on the ship's sonar. We arrived in Liverpool on D Day and I was sent to get additional transitional training in P51s which I would eventually fly in combat.

After twenty hours instruction in a P 51, I was assigned as a replacement pilot to the 364th Squadron of the 357th Fighter Group stationed in

Leiston, England. Our Base was located the farthest east of any of the fighter bases in the 8th Air Force and because of that location, we were most often assigned to escort the bombers at the further most sector of their penetration which usually was on their bomb run into their target. My first mission was to Stettin which was north of Berlin. It was a long mission which took over four hours.

I was asked to tell this story at air bases in England after my return to Allied Territory in order to brief pilots who were still flying combat missions in early 1945. It was thought that my experiences behind enemy lines might help combat pilots should they find themselves in similar circumstances.

Shortly after I was assigned to the 357th, I had heard a very interesting story by a Lieutenant Charles E. Yeager, who had just returned to our Group after being shot down behind enemy lines. He had evaded capture and had walked through France and escaped into Spain. Little did I know that several things he said then were to flash into my mind later just at the right time and save my life. At the time of his talk, I was confident that none of what he said was going to apply to me, but it must have embedded itself in my subconscious and I have thanked God ever since that it did.

On September 19, 1944 we took off to again fly protective cover for the transport planes and gliders that were dropping airborne troops into Holland near the city of Arnhem. We had completed a very successful mission similar to this one the day before, on September 18th. On that day, our Squadron had intercepted a group of German planes which we estimated to be between forty and fifty ME 109's and FW 190's. We were able to destroy at least twenty six of their planes without the loss of a single P51 due to enemy action. Had this group of enemy aircraft made contact with our transports, they would have added to the slaughter that was already taking place. As it was, the whole "Market Garden" mission was a disaster. Several thousand British troops were left stranded north of the Rhine near Arnhem where "The Bridge Too Far" was destroyed.

During the mission on September 18th, I had experienced my first contact with enemy aircraft. Previously, I had flown seventeen missions of escorting B17s, B24s, B26s, ground strafing convoys and skip bombing troop trains, but with no contact with the enemy other than flak.

On the mission of the eighteenth, on takeoff, I had advanced about halfway down the runway when my engine balked and just about cut out. I had lost all power so I throttled back and just managed to pull the plane into the air enough to clear the trees at the end of the runway. At normal climbing RPM's and manifold pressure my Rolls Royce Packard engine ran smoothly and after climbing slowly, we finally leveled off at 25,000 feet.

On that day our squadron was not leading the Croup and somehow we became separated from the 362nd and the 363rd. We had contact with radar control from England and had asked them for a vector on which we could rejoin our group. We were told that a large gaggle of planes were within their scope near us and they directed us on a collision course with what we thought were the rest of our P 51's. So naturally when we closed on them, we just pulled along side of them and momentarily ended up flying formation with about forty enemy aircraft.

I was flying the wing of our Squadron Leader, Lt. Shaw, and it wasn't until we had pulled into the enemy that I noticed the German crosses. My Squadron Leader slid in behind a 109. I stayed some distance off of his right wing but even with him so I could protect his rear. He opened fire just as I saw two 190's coming directly in on his tail. I called this information to him, and he rolled his ship over to his right directly towards me. I had to roll to the right likewise to avoid him and in so doing my left wing blocked him out. I continued to roll and pull back on the stick until I was in a 400 mile per hour dive straight for the ground.

I dropped my diving flaps and hauled back on the stick. I had no idea how many G's I pulled, but I was wearing a G suit and I could feel the air pockets forcing themselves against my legs. All of a sudden a 109 came into my sights at about a seventy degree angle. I pulled back harder until my Nydar Sight was on his canopy and squeezed the trigger. This was a Navy self-compensating sight that automatically took into consideration the necessary lead. White flashes soon appeared all over his canopy and I managed to roll out, next to the 109. I was so tight into his left side that I could see the flames in his cockpit and the blood oozing from his mouth – a ghastly sight – one that I saw many times later in my dreams.

Then his left wing slowly came up as his plane rolled over and he plunged straight down about 8,000 feet into the ground. I looked around and could not see any of their planes or ours. I thought that the action had been so brief that perhaps ray gun cameras had not picked up enough to confirm a "Destroyed." I turned my gun switch off, flew down to where the109 had gone in and made several passes at the wreckage with my camera on.

I had just pulled up from my last pass when I looked back and saw the big hub of a 190 right on my tail. I threw the throttle wide open for immediate extra power and my engine again balked, forcing me to pull back to 30 inches of mercury. I knew then that in no way could I climb or maneuver into position. I had just one chance – one thing I could do – fly as slow as I could in a tight turn to the right and stay as close to the ground as I dare go. I had heard that the FW 190 tends to snap under when attempting to do this maneuver. So I proceeded to go around-and-around about 50 feet off the ground. The 190 hung on my tail with his guns blazing, but he just couldn't pull up tight enough to get the proper lead on me.

Several farmers and women were running around on the ground directly under us. They were waving and no doubt did not realize the danger they were in. At one point, I put my hand on my head expecting a shell to blast through my canopy at any moment. I also did some fast praying. After several turns, I looked back and he was gone. I was alone. Slowly I climbed up to 10,000 feet and called

England. They vectored me into Brussels with instructions to land there.

By the time I reached Brussels, I was at 32,000 feet and figured that I could make it back over the Channel to my base. However, when I came in I did not do a "victory roll" as I buzzed the landing strip on my first approach because of the condition of my engine.

✔ Our normal landing procedure was to come in as low as possible on our initial approach directly over the landing strip, chop back completely on the throttle, and pull back on the stick in a tight climbing turn to the left. As our speed came down, we would continue to climb and turn until we were on our downwind leg. Then we would still continue to turn, but start to dive so that we could roll out just as we were about twenty feet above the beginning of the runway without having to use the throttle. Then it was just a matter of setting her down. Anybody who misjudged and had to go around a second time or chickened out and used some throttle, caught a lot of flak from any observers.

This time, I took wide, gentle turns to make sure that I would be able to set down on my first attempt and not have to gun the engine. After I cut the engine in my revetments, my crew chief hurriedly climbed up to the cockpit because he had seen that the tape was blown off the gun ports. I told him what had happened and he said, "Nice going, Lieutenant. I'll check out what's wrong." He actually worked all night and the next morning he reported to me that he could not see how I had ever kept the plane in the air. The plugs were that bad.

On the September 19th mission, we again flew cover for the landings in the Arnhem area. This time, I had the misfortune of having my flight becoming separated from the rest of the squadron. Also, one of the wingmen had aborted. The three of us were flying at about 15,000 feet when we were bounced by about forty 109's. It happened so fast that I had no idea where my flight leader or the other wingman disappeared to. I knew immediately that this was going to be rougher than the day before.

About twelve 109's ended up in a tight circle with me. I opened fire as I closed in on one ship and noticed parts of his plane coming off and smoke pouring out of his wing. I did not see him bail out. However, he slowly nosed over and plunged to the ground. I again tightened my turn and got in behind the second 109 and scored several hits on him. After a few more turns, I was able to pull up tighter on him and after a short burst of my six fifty caliber wing guns, his plane burst into flames.

In the meantime, there were two or three 109's who made head-on dives at me and then all of a sudden my left wing seemed to explode. The doors on the magazine racks popped open and the wing was in flames. I had to decide right then and there whether I should roll over and dive for the ground with the possibility of the rush of air putting out the fire, or whether I should bail out before the flames got to the wing tanks and blew the plane apart. I decided to bail out.

In a split second the words of Chuck Yeager came to me. "Put the plane in a tight climbing turn to the right. When you think you're about to stall, release the canopy, unfasten your safety belt, climb up and jump out on the inside of your turn. In that way you won't hit the tail assembly."

It worked! I was safely in the air and was rapidly beginning to gain speed in my fall. I was at about 18,000 feet when I jumped and again Yeager's words came back to me: "Don't by all means pull your rip cord. Your chute will open and the whole German Army will be waiting for you when you get to the ground." Plus, with Allied airborne troops landing in the same area, the German ground troops would shoot at anything in a chute. But, I was spinning – revolving so fast that I could not see how close the ground was coming up on me. Once more, the advice of Chuck popped into my head. "Spread your arms and legs. It will keep you face down so you can see." I gradually stopped spinning and finally there I was in a giant swan dive with my arms and legs outstretched. At about 1,200 feet, I decided to open my chute. First a little chute was released which then pulled out the big chute. There was a strong jerk on my harness when the air filled out the big chute. Then, I just sat there. The sky was blue – free of clouds. There was a large freshly plowed field directly below me. Everything seemed to be going right until I heard the whir of an inline engine and looked up to see a 109 coming in to strafe me.

How I knew to do it, I have no idea, but I quickly reached up and grabbed two shroud lines on one side of the chute and pulled myself up on them. This dumped some of the air out of the chute and I fell at a much more rapid pace. I evidently dropped out of the sights of the 109 and all his shots missed me. (Later I learned that some shot went into my chute.) He didn't make a second pass since I was getting very close to the ground.

When I was about 100 feet off the ground, I realized how fast I was descending. I tried to turn so that I would be facing towards the direction that I was drifting. I was going to land in the center of the field that had just been plowed. The soft dark brown earth cushioned my fall so that I was able to quickly unfasten my chute, gather it up and run to edge of the field. However, my "G" suit, which was very tight fitting, caused a cramp in my legs by the time I had run the thirty yards.

I buried my chute in the loose ground at the edge of the field and then crawled over to a small tobacco patch. I lay underneath the large leaves for what seemed to be a half hour, but it was probably no more than a few minutes.

After a while, the cramps left my legs and I got up into a kneeling position and looked around. I saw a small girl not more than forty feet away motioning for me to get down. She was pointing toward the next field where I saw a German soldier walking with his back to me. He had his gun in the ready position and no doubt had been sent out to search for me. I got down immediately and remained motionless.

About a half hour later, I crawled slowly through the large tobacco leaves until I reached a deep, narrow trench which was the drainage ditch between two adjacent fields. The trench was no more than two feet wide and yet it was over four feet deep and it was dry. The first thing I did was to take off the "G" suit, which was no easy operation in those tight quarters. I then lit a cigarette and decided to remain there until it became dark. I could hear a considerable amount of rifle and machine gun fire in the distance. There was also the intermittent concussion of exploding artillery and mortar shells.

Slowly darkness fell and after a short while I began to hear someone faintly whistling the code for the letter "V" in the distance. It became louder and louder as the person neared my position in the ditch. I debated whether it was a Dutchman who had come to help me or a German soldier who was cleverly trying to get me to reveal my hiding place. I finally risked raising my head above ground level and saw a young man who was saying softly, "American pilot, I am your friend." He would then whistle dit-dit-dit-da and repeat, "American pilot, I am your friend."

I decided that since I had my loaded 45 pistol, I would risk going up to him. He was very calm and pretended not to notice my gun pointed directly at him. Then in very broken English, he told me that he would help me to safety so I followed him. We had not gone too far before we were joined by another young man who walked with us to a farm house. We entered and suddenly I was standing in front of a group of Dutch men, women and several small children. They were all smiling and seemed very glad to see me. At that point I could not help it but I just burst into tears at the sight of these friends. I learned that the first young man's name was Gijs Jansen Van Beek and that we were at the home of John Emmerzaal, his friend.

On missions, we always carried an escape kit in our flight suits. It contained maps printed on rubberized silk, photographs for which we had posed in civilian clothes, a packet of water purification tablets and a number of other helpful items such as Dutch, French and German money, a water bag and a needle and thread. I opened the kit and gave Gijs all the money and my photographs. I offered everybody cigarettes and also gave John's mother two Hershey chocolate bars which I had tucked into the pocket of my flight jacket.

Neither the adults nor the young children could speak English. So, I could not understand any of their conversation. Occasionally Gijs or John would try to relate to me what had been said. After about an hour, Gijs and I left the farm house and proceeded to a church near the center of the little village of Angeren. We crossed fields, climbed over fences and finally entered the church through a back door. We climbed several flights of stairs and finally ended up in the steeple.

I was astounded how calm Gijs had been. His act of helping me was greatly endangering his life, but he acted boldly and without fear. Perhaps his bold action avoided arousing suspicion. I later learned that the knowledge of my whereabouts had to be kept from many of the Dutch neighbors as well as the Germans for fear of betrayal, weakness, or the tendency of most Dutch to talk too much. I was the seventh pilot that Gijs had helped including a wounded Canadian pilot that he took almost all the way to the Allied troops in Nijmegen.

When we were lying up in the steeple, Gijs whispered to me that down below that evening there would be several German officers staying in a small house about fifty feet from the church. While were whispering, I occasionally heard the conversation of the Germans down below. All this time, of course, the firing continued, and I thought for sure that I would be unable to sleep. But, as the tension left me, I dozed off.

It must have been about 4:00 a.m. when Gijs awakened me. We went down the way we had gone up, out the back door and started across the fields in a dense fog. I recall one time when we came to a fence he laboriously climbed over and I merely put my hand on the top of the post and vaulted over. Gijs remarked, "Good show," which no doubt was something he had heard on the BBC. He was very proud of his English, although I often had to ask him to repeat himself in order to understand just what he had said.

We must have traveled about a half a mile before arriving at the back of a house where I was to spend the next few days. Gijs opened the door and we entered the house of Antoon Stevens, who, Gijs told me, was the village policeman. At the time I saw him, he was not in his uniform. He greeted me heartily, as did his wife, his three sons and his three daughters. He escorted me into the front room and stood there like a small boy who had just been given a new toy.

He was very frustrated, however, since he could not speak English and I understood not one word of Dutch. I was able to speak a little German, as I had had two years of German in high school. This was to be our only way communicating. He had to figure out just what words I knew and try to reply accordingly, although sometimes he merely talked louder when I did not understand. Mr. Steven's sons could speak English about as well as Gijs, and I often had to tell one of them and he would then translate to the family.

For the first two or three days I was given cigarettes and we had very wonderful meals. However, Mr. Stevens asked me to sleep in the hayloft, which was in the rear portion of the house. He had the fear that perhaps at night somebody might unexpectedly enter the house and discover me. He told me that if that happened, he and his family would certainly be promptly marched out of the house and shot.

On the afternoon of the third day while I was sitting in the front living room, I heard the heavy concussion of artillery fire from the south. I could also hear the eerie drone of shells as they passed overhead. About the third volley, the approaching shells built up to such a terrific whine that I was certain that they were not going to pass over and would probably hit close to the house. I dove for the floor. One of the shells struck the house directly across the street and practically blew up a woman. Parts of the shrapnel flew across the street and shattered the living room window. I recall that as I lay there, a piece of shrapnel landed about two feet from me. I reached over to pick it up and dropped it immediately. It was red hot. After the firing ceased, there was silence except for the screaming coming from what was left of the house across the street.

On the fourth day, I was sitting in the living room when all of a sudden a man in a black uniform entered the room. I immediately concluded that this was a member of the Gestapo or a German officer. I did not look close enough to see that it was Mr. Stevens in his policeman's uniform. He burst into laughter until the tears rolled down his cheeks at the expression of shock on my face.

On September 23rd, my birthday, John Emmerzaal came into the house with a box under his arm. He carefully opened it and took out a cake with chocolate frosting. At this point I did not realize what chocolate meant to these Dutch people. I was unaware of how severe the Nazi oppression had been for nearly five years. John told me how his mother had made the frosting out of the candy bars I had given her. Rather than enjoy this treasure themselves, they decided to make me a very special cake because they knew I would miss the celebration I would have had at home.

The Dutch people consider a birthday as a great occasion. I was given several packs of special cigarettes and we sampled a variety of liqueurs. All the Stevens family and others who visited while I was there looked at me as a hero who had come to liberate them. Although they knew I was no longer able to do much good in the effort, somehow or other, I must have symbolized those who they hoped and prayed would come shortly and free them.

In the morning of the 24th of September, Mr. Stevens rushed into the room where I was sitting and told me that the Germans had moved several pieces of artillery into the backyard and that I would have to move upstairs and remain hidden in a small space under the eve of the roof. There was a good chance that the soldiers would be moving in and out of the lower rooms of the house and it would be too dangerous for me as well as his family if I were to remain in the living room.

Mr. Stevens took me upstairs into one of the bedrooms and removed a panel from the wall. At that point, the roof was about three feet above the floor and the space was only two feet wide. As I crawled into the dark hole, he told me to remain absolutely quiet and he would open the panel in a few hours. I had considerable difficulty when I wanted to turn around and I thought my bladder would burst by the time Mr. Stevens and his son, Bernhard, returned with a small pot. He allowed me just enough time to relieve myself. He then hurried me back under the eaves and replaced the panel. I stayed in there all day and all night with only brief moments outside for hastily cramming down food and taking a drink of water. Mr. Stevens watched the stairway up to the attic area while I relieved myself. He was very frightened. The next morning Mr. Stevens thought it was too much of a hardship on me and decided that I could remain in the bedroom. Yet that evening, he became so frightened at a new turn of events that he rushed me outside of the house and placed me in a tobacco patch about fifty yards from the rear of the house. It was raining and the only protection I could find was under the tobacco leaves. After about an hour, I heard artillery fire opening up from the south and again I heard the whining of the approaching shells. Then the whine grew louder and louder and I knew the shells were going to hit near the tobacco patch. That was the first time I realized what the infantry soldier had to go through. I lay flat on the ground and I clawed at it and tried to dig into it, hoping that in some fantastic way I could pull myself into it. I knew the shells were hitting nearby and the shrapnel was zinging over my head and landing near me. I pressed myself down as flat as I could and prayed.

Suddenly it stopped and all I could hear was the rain as it fell on the tobacco leaves. I was wet and shaking and unable to sleep at all. I could only wait for dawn and the rain to stop. I knew I could not move until Mr. Stevens would come to get me.

Just after it started to get light, he came out to me with a blanket. He motioned me to follow him and we took off in a direction away from the house. We had gone about three hundred yards, and he stopped at a fairly large ditch. He told me to get in the bottom of the ditch under the bushes. He then handed me a package of cigarettes and sortie matches and said he would come back later with food. That's all he said and then he disappeared.

I lay on my stomach, rolled up in the blanket in the bottom of the ditch. I was fairly well screened by a thick growth of bushes that lined both sides. I had just finished my second cigarette when I heard a faint swishing sound. The sound grew louder and then there was a muffled explosion and then silence. I stood up and tried to see what had happened. I could see nothing and had dropped to my hands and knees when I heard someone running towards me. I froze in that position. The footsteps came closer and I realized that somebody was running along the ditch. I could hear my heart pounding in my eardrums as the person running stopped with his foot not eighteen inches from my right hand. Out of the corner of my eye I had seen the hobnails on the bottom of his left boot as his last footstep came down. He had stopped directly next to me and I assumed he had seen me. He said nothing, but then I heard another soldier on my left shout "nach hinden" which meant "back farther." Then the soldier standing over me moved off to the south, never knowing how close he had just been to one of his enemies. This was the first of many encounters I was to have with German soldiers during my stay in Holland.

About four o'clock that afternoon Mr. Stevens came with a dish of food and told me that if he could he would return that evening. If not, he would see me in the morning. I ate the meal slowly so that I could relish every taste. I lay in the ditch without moving other than to turn from one side to the other. Mr. Stevens did not return and all that night the Allied shelling continued. However, their target was not as close as it was my first night in the tobacco patch.

In the morning, Mr. Stevens came out with his son, Bernard, and motioned to me to follow him. Bernard explained as we walked that his father had decided that even though it would be very risky he could not stand to think what I was going through lying out in the ditch. He felt I should come and stay with them in the house and that his family was willing to take the chance that I would not be noticed. The German field pieces had been moved out as they did not stay in one position longer than twenty four hours. Allied photo-recon planes would pick them up and that would invite immediate counter shelling.

So, I again moved into the Stevens house. Only this time I slept with the family in the cellar. This only lasted for two days.

On the twenty eighth of September an ultimatum was given to the residents of Angeren by the Germans. They were told that they must move out within forty eight hours. Because of their closeness to the front lines, the Germans feared sabotage and, of course, they could then freely loot their houses and butcher their livestock.

Mr. Stevens' family first moved about four hundred yards to the east to the farmhouse of a friend from whom he knew he could borrow a sizable wagon and a horse. The two families had decided they would move out together in the morning and cross the Rhine River. Gijs was to go with them since his family had moved out several days earlier because Germans had taken over their farm house.

I made up my mind to stay there hoping that the Allies would move forward just those ten or eleven miles that separated me from freedom. Gijs told me of a small barn in the orchard about three hundred meters further to the east. He told me that he had housed two Belgium boys there for several days. They had escaped from a German work camp and were trying to get back home.

The following morning Mr. Stevens and Gijs took me out to the barn. Gijs went out a short distance with a pail and milked one of the cows that was roaming in the orchard. In the meantime, Mr. Stevens, before saying goodbye, gave me two packs of cigarettes and handed me two identification documents.

One, he explained, was what the Germans called an "Ausweis" for an "H. B. Jansen" and the other was a card declaring that the same "H. B. Jansen" was declared to be deaf and dumb by an institute in Maastricht, Holland, which was already in Allied hands. Therefore that document could not be disputed. The "Ausweis" or identification folder was a document that all Dutch people had to carry on their person and present upon demand to any German who asked for it. Mr. Stevens went to great lengths to instruct me on how to act deaf and dumb. He had retrieved one of the photos that I had handed out the first night in Emmerzaal's farmhouse. He had found an artist in town who had hand drawn very skillfully the document declaring that I, H. B. Jansen, was deaf and dumb and he had also refurbished a previously issued "Ausweis" and had changed it to now contain the identity of the same H. B. Jansen (me) by carefully placing my photo where the real H. B. Jansen's photo had been removed. The artist then redrew in purple ink on my photo the portion of the official German stamp that had originally been placed half on Jansen's photo so that it again fit perfectly with the other half that had remained on the document. Mr. Stevens explained that one page in the false document could not be repaired and he hoped that no one would examine that page too closely and discover the error.

I will never forget when he gave me the documents. He went through all sorts of antics and muttered gibberish and moaned to show how he thought one who was deaf and dumb would try to communicate. At the time, I thought it all very silly. Little did I know that within twenty four hours I would be putting on the same act. Only then it would be before a very critical German audience and I would have to be convincing.

After Mr. Stevens and Gijs had left, I was alone, totally alone and the fear of what might lie ahead for me made me pray for help and strength to be able to get back home safely. There was very little food and no water. I could find cows to milk every day, but because of their not having been milked regularly twice a day, the milk had formed a large ball that remained in the cows' udders and all I got was nothing more than a very thin liquid – not milk. However, it must have had some food value and it did quench my thirst. Of course, I was in an orchard containing several varieties of apples and pears still on the streets. But, thin milk and fruit did not begin to replace a warm meal. This diet started me on a weight loss program of about thirty five pounds or more over the next few weeks.

On the first afternoon of my stay in the barn, I looked around the premises and found a small room in a back corner of the barn in which there was a hole leading to a short tunnel. This, no doubt, was where the two Belgium boys went when they wanted to avoid detection by an intruder. I also climbed a ladder to a loft and found a small German trench shovel and a canister containing a discarded chemical warfare kit. In looking through the kit, I found a small case sealed with adhesive tape. I carefully removed the tape and used it to seal the open end of a plastic envelope in which I placed the good side of the identification with my photo facing out and my deaf and dumb document on the other side. Now the important part of both documents could be examined with less danger of the mutilated page being seen unless the examiner took time to peel back the tap and take both documents out of the plastic enclosure.

The first night, I decided to sleep in the tunnel. I crawled down into the hole and found a candle in the tunnel. I wasn't down there more than ten minutes before I was overcome by the closeness of the walls and damp musty smell. I felt I would be better off sleeping up on the floor of the barn where I could breathe and not feel that the walls were closing in on me. I reasoned that the soldiers would not be wandering around at night examining deserted barns. They would be too fearful of the chance of running into an Allied patrol. Perhaps in the daytime, I could make a hasty retreat to the safety of the tunnel should someone approach the barn.

So, I lay down and stretched out on the straw on the floor. Within five minutes, I heard a good deal of rustling and scratching all around me. The rats too, evidently, were hiding from the Germans. I ended up sleeping a short time and then flailing my arms out so the rats would know that I did not intend to be their evening warm meal. This would cause them to retreat far enough to give me time to catch a few winks and then I'd repeat the process.

The next morning, I went out and milked two cows that were within fifty yards of the barn. I also picked several apples and then returned to my "mansion." I had drunk all the milk and after finishing an apple I placed the remaining apples under the pail in the small room. I was looking out into the orchard through one of the cracks between the siding on the barn when all of a sudden the door swung open and two German soldiers walked into the barn.

For a moment, they looked as surprised as I am sure I did. Right then I realized that this was my first curtain call. My fear must have made me put on a convincing performance – one that would have made Mr. Stevens proud of me. The two soldiers were impressed or at least convinced that I was deaf and dumb and hungry. I could translate just enough of what they were saying in German to each other to detect that they wanted to take me to their field kitchen for a warm meal.

With many hand signals and considerable muttering, I finally convinced them that I wanted to stay in the barn. One had just taken a bite out of an apple and he felt so sorry for me that he handed it to me hoping it would help. After they had waved goodbye and left, I fell on the floor and laughed out loud at my success. This gave me some confidence in the documents and my acting ability, thanks to the explicit tutoring of Mr. Stevens. By this time something was building inside of me. It was the positive thought that I would get home. Little by little the sequence of what was happening – the perfect timing of the "right prior input" and then the subsequent "call-to-action of that input" seemed more than coincidental. Somebody – not just the Dutch – was helping me. And, as this scenario kept repeating itself, little doubt was left in my mind that that "Some-body" was hearing my prayers and that he was not just building up my hopes only to have something go wrong later that would prevent me from ever reaching freedom.

Each day I was able to locate the herd of cows in the orchard and managed to get sufficient milk and along with a few apples or pears I was able to sustain myself – keep up my energy level. However, I could see that I was losing weight every day.

On my third day in the barn, I ran out of tobacco and no longer could roll cigarettes. Smoking was vital to my life or at least I thought so. I remember how I could hardly wait to get down below ten thousand feet when returning from a high altitude escort mission so that I could take off my oxygen mask and light up a cigarette. Since I knew where the last farmer's house was, the one where Mr. Stevens had picked up the wagon, I decided to make my way there and search the buildings. In order to avoid being seen, I crawled the two block distance up a shallow ditch. On the way, I came upon some very large carrots still in the ground. I put several of them in my jacket pocket. When I got to the house, I looked in every room, every garment pocket, every container and a small low shed in the rear. In the shed, I found green leaves of tobacco hanging to dry from the ceiling rafters. I pulled them down and bundled them up. In the pockets of garments hanging on the walls I found twenty four matches. I also found three pullet eggs in a nest in the tobacco shed. I then decided to get back to the shed as fast as I could.

Later, I realized that the house might have been booby trapped and that I had just blundered all over it with little concern of the potential danger. I also had to cross to the far side of the orchard before I came to the ditch. This made me very visible for quite a distance in several directions. This brought me to the conclusion that in the future, I would have to think things out more carefully before I just charged into the unknown. God could do a lot, but I had to help.

I opened the eggs. Two were fresh and I ate them raw. The other one was rotten. I also ate one of the carrots. Then I tightly rolled up one of the large tobacco leaves and thinly sliced it into cigarette size tobacco. Using part of another leaf, I was able to roll a cigar size cigarette. I lit it and found that I had to continually puff on it to keep it going because of the greenness of the leaves. Not good, but better than nothing. Besides, it kept me busy and took away some of my hunger pains.

Every day I carved the day and the date into one of the timbers in the barn. Also, in order to pass the time until the Allies would come, I carved little figures out of pieces of a board I had found.

By the sixth day I was very, very hungry. My stool was a milky white and the carrots had gone straight through me, totally undigested. Previously, I had observed a large pig and her young roaming in the orchard. I just happened to be looking out when, to my surprise, the sow flopped down not fifteen feet from the door of the barn and the piglets immediately crawled all over her belly until each had located an open feeding station. Her head was away from the barn so she could not see the door. I picked up the small shovel and slowly opened the door. Then I rushed out and grabbed one of the little pigs by his two hind legs. The sow and the rest of her brood quickly scurried away. I held the piglet's head on the ground and swung the shovel. The blade slashed through its neck and it stopped squealing. It didn't move. It had been killed instantly and I took it inside the barn and closed and latched the door.

I was excited. The violent activity and the thought of finally having something to eat made my heart pound. I sat down and just waited until I had calmed down. I also thought of how and when I was going to cook the piglet. During the day, the smoke would certainly be noticed. At night, the fire would be observed since I could not take a chance of having the fire in the barn. The straw would surely catch fire and burn the barn down. Plus, I kept looking at the little pig and the feeling of remorse started to grow and replace my thoughts of dinner. I finally gave up the idea of a nice pork roast and buried the little guy in the ground floor of the barn. On the eighth day, I was sitting in the barn and heard several voices. I ran to that side of the barn and through the slits between the boards I could see a group of boys and a German soldier about thirty yards away walking through the orchard. With the direction they were traveling they would pass directly in front of the barn. I put the latch down , and went into the back room and waited. One of the boys decided to investigate the barn and began pulling violently on the door in an effort to break in. Finally the latch gave and the door swung open.

I had made up my mind that I did not want to meet him on the inside so I started walking through the doorway muttering and moaning. This frightened the daylights out of him and he ran back to join the others. The German soldier immediately pulled out his luger and ran towards me. He continued to hold his gun on me as I showed him my identification cards in the plastic holder. Finally, he took it, looked at it for a moment, and then handed it to one of the Dutch boys. After a bit, the boy explained that I was deaf and dumb. The soldier thought for a minute and then made signs to me that I should get my belongings and join them. I packed up my carvings and what little tobacco I had left in an extra pair of overalls. It was about one o'clock in the afternoon when I left my home in the orchard.

I was frightened to be in the hands of a German soldier, but felt some comfort with the presence of the Dutch boys and that my papers and my "presentation" seemed to have again passed the test.

The balance of the afternoon I spent as an assistant to one of the boys who skinned and dressed out pigs. Another group caught and killed them. Later the Germans came around with a light truck, picked up the carcasses and hauled them back to their field kitchen.

After we had done this for about four hours, we all sat down in a small wooded grove to rest. The soldier sat down and leaned back against a tree to make himself comfortable. Somehow I sensed that he was not quite satisfied with just the brief examination of my identification cards and that he would soon search me more thoroughly. I moved a short distance away and kneeled down behind a tree in the pretense of relieving myself. I quickly took my silver identification bracelet, my flight watch, and my dog tags and slipped them in a crack between the trunk of the tree and the surrounding sod. It wasn't ten minutes later before he called me over by motioning with his arm when he saw I was looking in his direction. After quite a thorough search he called one of the Dutch boys to him. After giving him some brief instructions, the boy left us and I wondered at the time whether this all had something to do with me. I slowly moved back to the tree and again pretended to relieve myself. Instead, I retrieved my watch. That, I could possibly indicate, I had found. The other two items would be dead giveaways, so I left them there.

A short time later, the boy returned with another Dutch boy who was about twelve years old. The soldier indicated that I was to go with this Dutch boy and that I would be taken care of and fed. We left and went some distance before we came to a large, nice looking house. We entered and I was surprised to find a large group of people staying on after the order had been issued that all Dutch people in Angeren had to leave that area. There was Mrs. Kok, the owner of the house and the mother of Ludwig, the boy who had brought me there. There was her other son, Dicki, and two daughters, Dini and Cori, all of whom were younger than Ludwig.

There were Mrs. Kok's mother and her father. There also were two additional families – eighteen in all.

They all treated me very kindly. No doubt because I was deaf and dumb. I was haggard looking because I was thin and had a fairly long beard. I never revealed to any of them that I was an American pilot. There were too many people, too many children, and too many German soldiers continually walking in and out of the house or coming in after dark to visit and eat treats that Mrs. Kok gave them or to play the piano and sing. It just would have been too risky to trust that neither an adult nor a child would not mistakenly give away my identity. Plus, if I were to be discovered by the Germans, how could they ever explain my being there without endangering their own lives.

I stayed with these people for seven days. I slept on the second floor and they all slept in the basement. Almost every night we could hear the shelling coming from the Allied troops in the south towards Nijmegen. Several nights the shells landed near the house. One blew the roof off of the cow barn.

During the shelling, I would have to wait until someone would have the courage to crawl up the stairs and wake me to tell me to follow them down to the cellar because of the danger. Little did they know that each time I was already quite awake and shaking in bed until they got there.

Every day, German soldiers would come into the house and Mrs. Kok would give them milk from the six cows she kept in the barn. She evidently was allowed to remain there so the soldiers could have the fresh milk.

The food that was prepared was very meager and consisted primarily of potatoes. I had noticed on the day that I was butchering with the Dutch boys that some of the fields still had a crop of Brussels sprouts or other vegetables in them. I often wondered why they didn't prepare something else to go along with all the potatoes.

One day, three German soldiers brought over some pork kidneys and livers. Evidently it was part of the pig that they did not care for and after eating it for two days I could see why. The Dutch people ate it with great relish, but I was sure that I would never be able to eat liver again.

One night, six very young German soldiers came in after dark and sat around the large table in the living room. The room contained several more chairs, a piano, and a fireplace. The fireplace was used to do all the cooking since there was no electricity to operate the stove. One of the soldiers played the piano and the others sang. There was one sullen looking dark-haired soldier that wanted to see my "Ausweis." I handed it over to him, but I could not take my eyes off of him for fear that he would look inside. He looked it all over carefully and started to pick the tape with his fingernail so he could pull it off. Just then Mrs. Kok brought came in with a jar of cherry preserves as a treat and he handed the envelope back to me. What timing! How lucky could I be!

The soldier who was playing the piano started up a lively tune and I got up and walked over and put my head against the side of the piano. I smiled and they all smiled, thinking it remarkable that I could hear or feel the vibrations. What a ham!

All in all, they seemed like a nice bunch of fellows. They were trying to have fun and I am sure they were reminded of the fun they used to have at home. Three of them admitted in answer to Mrs. Kok's questioning that they still had their religious beliefs despite the Nazi doctrine they recently had been taught. There were moments that I almost forgot that they were my enemies.

I had to be extremely cautious so as not to become noticeably startled by any distracting sound.

One afternoon, when I was in a field in back of the house, I heard a single rifle shot. I whipped my head around just when one of the farmers happened to be looking at me. He smiled a little and we went back in the house. I never could figure out just what had gone through his mind. He knew I wasn't deaf. He didn't know that I was an American. Maybe he thought that I was just a Dutchman trying to avoid being hauled off to Germany to work in a labor camp. Since I noticed no change in the attitude of the others, I deducted that he had told no one of what he had seen that afternoon.

At the time I had gone on the pig skinning expedition, my right index finger had been deeply cut when the knife of the skinner slipped as he was separating the skin that I was pulling on from the flesh. I also had received several cuts on my face when one of the farmers tried to shave me with a dull rusty open razor. I stopped him because of the damage he was doing and it came to me that I needed the beard to help hide my age. I was twenty seven at the time. These wounds became infected and soon I had a rapidly spreading case of impetigo on my face and my hand and wrist. I forgot to mention that when I had bailed out of my airplane, I had ripped a chunk out of my wrist somehow. It must have caught on something. It never really closed up and the infection from my finger had also found its way to the sore on my wrist.

At this point I had lost about thirty pounds and the beard gave me a gaunt look which made the Dutch people refer to me as "the old man."

In the morning of the seventh day of my stay with the Koks, while I was sitting in the living room, two officers entered the room and the one with the most braid on his cap started shouting at Mrs. Kok, asking why she was still there and that she should pack up and get out by nine o'clock the next morning or they would all be shot. After they had stomped out, everybody started to pack on Mrs. Kok's instructions.

By evening a wagon was loaded to the limit. In the morning, a horse was hitched in place and two cows and one heifer were tied to the rear of the wagon. Everybody had put on extra clothing. I had found a set of "clumpers" (wooden shoes) and I thought that by wearing them I would really look Dutch. What I didn't know was that if they didn't fit perfectly, they would hurt tender feet and cause blisters.

After a light breakfast, the entire entourage of eight adults, ten children, and one American pilot departed from the house at eight o'clock. We left the town of Angeren and headed east on a very huge dike along the Rhine river.

The clumpers kept my feet warm and dry and I was able to keep up with the slow moving wagon. We walked several miles on the dike until we came to a ferry that was to take us across the Rhine River. It consisted of a platform over eight barges lashed side-to-side behind eight more barges also lashed side-to-side. There were four outboard motors fastened to the rear that would slowly push the whole contraption along a guide cable that stretched across the river. After the wagon was pulled onto the center of the ferry, we all walked on as did about twenty German soldiers. They did not talk to any of us and after the ferry docked we pulled up on another dike on the other side and started our trek to the north.

We covered about twelve miles the first day and in late afternoon we stopped at the farmhouse of a friend of the Kok's. The two farmers butchered the heifer and we enjoyed a roast beef dinner that evening.

That night I became ill, very ill. I had dysentery and all the discomfiture that went with it. The impetigo was spreading, and the wooden shoes had worn a large blister on my left foot. They had also caused a good deal of swelling across the insteps of both of my feet. All that plus weakness from the loss of weight made me feel quite miserable. The fresh killed beef went straight through me and handling that in a crowd was not easy. That morning I made gestures to Mrs. Kok that I was very sick and she motioned for me to climb on the wagon and ride with her father and her mother. The rest all walked as we again headed north.

We crossed a very large bridge early in the morning that I noted had guard houses at both ends. However, they did not bother to query us as to where we were going. One time, we passed a group of soldiers that I estimated to be at least four hundred. They were sitting on the side of a hill, singing songs. They seemed to be singing to us as we passed directly in front of them. They sang very well and very loud. Perhaps many of them were just as homesick as I was. Of course, they had no idea who was in their audience.

I had a constant fear that we would be stopped and each one questioned by one of the numerous German officers or soldiers we passed along the way. Although there were nineteen individuals in the group, I couldn't get it out of my mind that it had to be obvious that I was different from the rest – that I was not Dutch.

That afternoon, we were going through the small town of Hummel and a miracle happened. On the corner of one of the streets, *I saw John Emmerzaal*, the young boy who had helped Gijs take me to his farm the first evening. The others also recognized him and we stopped. I slid down off the wagon and managed to get to him first. I quickly told him how sick I was and that I had to see a doctor immediately or give myself up to the Germans in order to get medical attention. He said he would help me and that I should wait with the Kok's until he contacted me.

What a remarkable coincidence! At just the right moment, he was there where I could see him – that he had gone to the same town that I was passing through. Somebody had made it happen – just that way and I knew who it was.

John told Mrs. Kok where to park the wagon and that he would be back after a short time. After a while he came out of the house we were parked in front of and motioned for me to follow him back into the house. We went into a sitting room and he then told me that he would take me to a doctor. Then he went out and told Mrs. Kok that I would be leaving them and perhaps they would want to say goodbye. He did not tell them who I was.

First, Mrs. Kok came in. I hugged her and gave her a kiss on her cheek. I could see that her eyes were starting to fill with tears and one rolled down her cheek. After she left, her mother came in. Before we left the house in Angeren I had given her a small wrapped and sealed Package to keep for me. She had put it in a small bag that she hung under her dress. Now she took out the bag and returned the small package. I also gave her a kiss on the cheek and then she left. The rest did not come in.

I pulled the curtain back slightly and watched as they moved on. When John returned, I opened the package and gave my flight watch to him. He told me that we would now go to the doctor's office — to a man, he was sure, would be able to help me.

We walked about a block and a half up the same street and entered his office. There were two men in the room, one older and one about my age. After the older one had gone out of the room, the younger man said to me in perfect English, "I am Dr. Ewout Van Der Weg. May I see your identification papers, please?" I handed them to him and after a brief look he said, "Please come over here under the light so I can examine you."

He looked at all of my infected areas and then went out of the room for a few minutes. When he returned, he was carrying one bottle of medicine and a jar. He handed them both to me and said, "This is for your health."

Then he picked up my identification envelope and handed it to me saying, "This is for your life."

Then he said, "I would like you to stay with me and my wife. We have no children. You will be safe there and we will be able to nurse you back to health. We will leave in a few minutes. I have two bicycles. It is not far. Perhaps you should say goodbye to John now. You will not be seeing him again."

Then he removed his white jacket as I said good-bye and thanked John for all he had done.

After John left, we went out the back door and got on the two bicycles that were standing there. I followed him. He did not go fast since he knew how weak I was. We finally were at the outskirts of town and heading up a gravel road towards a large building that looked like a castle. We went to the back of the building and put the bikes in a shed and after the doctor had padlocked the shed, we entered the building through the back door. A long hall led to a stairway that took us up to the second floor. We walked down another hall and stopped in front of the first door. The Doctor knocked. I heard a voice inside and then the Doctor said very clearly, "It is me" and then I could hear the latch being turned. The door opened. A woman stood in the doorway. She was about five feet three inches tall. She had blondish hair and intense blue eyes.

The Doctor said, "Howard, this is my wife, Miep."

She looked at me and back to him. She said something in Dutch and then looked back at me, smiled, and said, "Please do come in."

I entered the room in which I was to stay for the next three months. I never left it except to go to the bathroom and one time to help Wout cut wood in the shed. The room had several easy chairs, a small dining table with four chairs, a small wood stove, a long bookcase the full length of one wall, and a cot pushed under one of the front windows. Two lamps were turned on as it now was dusk outside and Miep had drawn the blackout shutters. There was fire in the stove.

Miep was an incessant chatterbox. She was so full of life and emotion – a complete contrast to her husband. He was always very calm. Nothing seemed to ever bother him. He truly was a remarkable man –

about six feet tall, slender, deep blue eyes, short wavy sand colored hair, and unusually small hands. He was very considerate of his wife. He loved her very much and constantly gave in to her every wish. She was three months pregnant with their first child. They were both my age, twenty seven. He could speak seven languages. He spoke German so fluently that often the German to whom he might be talking would think he was one of them.

Miep's English was amusing. Most times it came out backwards and she talked so fast that I had difficulty understanding her at first. She too was a graduate Doctor, but had given up her practice.

About six o'clock Miep went out of the room and returned shortly with several bowls and small platter of meat. She had already set the table and we sat down to a very delicious dinner.

Earlier, Wout had given me some medicine to start curing the dysentery and had smeared a black paste that looked like grease over areas affected by the impetigo. After dinner, he showed me the toilet off of the landing that was half way up the stairs we had climbed earlier.

The house was owned by Mrs. Markvoort and was called "The Villa Johanna." She and her late husband had run the very large farm and had raised their family in the Villa. She now lived alone and her son ran the farm. She had rented the small section that we were in to the Doctor and his wife. Mrs. Markvoort did most of the cooking and supplied the fruits and vegetables. The Doctor on his rounds to the farmers quite often was paid with meat, poultry, or sausage, which was then turned over to Mrs. Markvoort to prepare. This combination of supply afforded us far better meals than most of the rest of the Dutch people. In urban areas, the Dutch were already starving since nothing was moving to the markets.

Every morning of my entire stay, Miep served me breakfast in bed. It usually consisted of small open faced sandwiches of apple or jelly or leftover meat. I would always have coffee and for the first week, I had eggs and rice. I later learned from Wout that the rice had been saved for the baby, but they thought I needed it more if I was to get well. Until the dysentery left, all fruits had to be peeled and the milk I drank was first boiled.

The first Saturday I was there, Miep handed me clean underwear, a shirt, pants, and socks, and took me down the hallway outside our room to the bathroom. She had already filled the huge iron tub with steaming hot water. She left me there and I immediately removed all of my clothes. I had not had my underwear off of my body since I had put it on back in England. I slowly climbed into the tub and sank down in was water until it came just below my chin. I was in heaven. I felt like I was being born again. I had to keep my infected right hand and wrist out of the water and also the large infected area on my face. I wanted desperately to dunk my head under the water. However, I did manage to wash my greasy, filthy hair without getting my face wet and when I climbed out of the tub I felt like a new man.

After putting on the wonderful, clean clothing, I returned to the room and Miep gave me a safety razor. I went into their bedroom and hacked off my beard and combed my hair. The mirror now revealed that I was no longer "the old man."

As our trust of each other strengthened, Miep told me that Wout was the head of the local underground, and later I met several of the agents who operated under his direction. However, when certain agents would visit, I would be asked to remain quietly in the bed-room until they had left. Wout had learned not to trust everybody, even some of those who professed their loyalty to his group. In that way, he could control who did and who did not know that I was staying in his house. If too many people knew, idle talk or a slip of the tongue to the wrong person could be fateful to all of us.

Some of the agents were only known or referred to by some identifying mark or characteristic such as "the man with the golden tooth" or "the big one." This was done so that the agent's real name would not be known and therefore he would not be able to be revealed by a "quisling."

One of those agents, Joseph, I saw fairly often since he visited Wout frequently. *He, Wout, and Gijs were three of the bravest men I have ever met.* Every time Joseph came to the Villa, he brought me tobacco or cigarettes. He was twenty one years old, about six feet four inches tall and had black, wavy hair. He was built like an ox and was ideally suited for the job he had with the underground. He was their exterminator. When a traitor or a "quisling" was discovered, he was given the assignment to kill that person as soon as possible.

He admired me very much since I was a pilot, something that he always wanted to be. While he was in the Dutch Merchant Marine, two ships he had sailed on had each been torpedoed and now he had the job of killing those that would betray their fellow countrymen just to gain, comfort with the enemy... He was an important member and yet he felt left out.

He wanted people to know what he was doing to help the effort of the underground, but instead, he had to keep a low profile and avoid associating with the others in his group. His usefulness depended on his remaining unknown so his presence would not cause alarm when he was about to carry out an assignment.

One evening, he came in with Wout and sat down in a chair and started to talk to me while Wout took off his coat and opened his satchel.

Wout then called over to him in Dutch, "Well, let me see it."

Joseph then removed his coat and rolled up the sleeve of his shirt. He had been shot by a German and the bullet passed clean through the fleshy part of his left arm just above the elbow. The German had shouted for him to stop, but Joseph at that time could not afford to be interrogated so he ran and the German shot. Joseph managed to escape and hid outside the Villa until Wout came home.

Wout cleaned the wound and then put a bandage on both sides of Joseph's arm. He then rolled down his sleeve, put on his coat and left.

I had been there about a month when the Germans moved a regiment through that area and billeted some of them in the Villa. They stayed on the first floor overnight. Only one officer came up the stairs and knocked on the door. After Wout opened it, he took about two steps in and looked around. He said nothing and seemed to be satisfied. He said "Dankaschoen" and returned to the first floor.

Later that evening, Mrs. Markvoort came up and told Wout that one of the soldiers were starting to build a fire on the living room floor. He hurried out and was able to find a mounted German officer. The officer rode to the Villa and thrashed the soldier with his riding crop right in front of Mrs. Markvoort as if to convince her that the Germans really didn't want to antagonize Dutch people.

Wout also told me that one day a German soldier stopped him and tried to take his bicycle away. A German officer happened to pass at the same time and when Wout told the officer what was going on and that he was a doctor and very much needed his bicycle, the officer also thrashed the soldier with his riding crop for "being so stupid" as Wout overheard.

In the second week in December, we had a visit from two American pilots who had come down in a B 26 from the Ninth Air force. The plane had been hit and the crew was instructed to bail out. The pilot and the co-pilot decided to ride the plane clown and landed it dead-stick in a farmers field. They were being sheltered in a small barge on a canal about ten kilometers east of us. They stayed overnight and we had a great time telling each other our experiences. We knew we would meet again since we were told that the underground would move us out together when the right time came.

They came back for a two day stay over Christmas. We all received packages of Turkish cigarettes and special candy. Mrs. Markvoort made a special dinner and we all got a little bombed on Dutch gin.

Occasionally, I would hear of groups of the underground who were discovered by the Gestapo and most times they were executed. One time three agents came in with a box containing six boxes of ammunition and eight new pistols. Wout examined them and then they were taken to be hidden in the chicken coop behind the Villa. They were to be used when the Allies advanced to take that area. The agents would have some means of resistance against any last minute atrocities by the retreating Germans.

One time for about a week, I drew maps of the fortifications in the Hummelo area. There were several anti-aircraft guns, V-1 launching sites, and two supply depots.

Almost every other night, we would hear the sputter of the V-1's going quite low over the house headed for Antwerp. The Germans had fled from Antwerp failing to demolish the docks and unloading facilities that were now being used by the Allies. The exploding buzz bombs were not accurate enough to do much precise damage, but they were occasionally hitting their targets.

The older man I had seen in Wout's office was Doctor Westerbeek, his associate. He had read a considerable amount of books in English and he made his entire collection available to me. Wont brought me a steady supply which helped to fill my time. At night, we listened to the BBC and quite often Wout challenged me to a game of chess. As I recall, I never beat him in a single game. He always won.

In the first week of February, I was told that plans had been made for me and the two other pilots to try to reach the Allies. On the night before I was to move out, the other two pilots spent the night with us in preparation of our leaving the following evening. At dusk, we assembled behind the Villa Johanna. We all had bicycles and two Dutch young men as well as Joseph joined us. He was given a 7mm Erfert pistol and was to lead. I rode in the rear and also carried an Erfert. The two pilots and I had key maps sewn into our coats. It started to drizzle as the six of us rode single file towards the south.

We moved down the same roads that I had come north on when retreating with the Koks. This drizzle kept the German soldiers indoors and off the streets and roads, so we were able to move without drawing attention. Finally, we came to the huge bridge that I remembered crossing with the Koks when we moved North. We all stopped and Joseph warned us that there was a guard house at each end of the bridge. If we were stopped, he would shoot the guard since we would all be shot if they discovered our identity and the pistols and maps. We were to move as fast as possible over the remainder of the bridge. We then proceeded up toward the first guard house. The rain fell more heavily. It seemed like forever to get there. Finally, there it was. We all pedaled slowly and quietly past it. We then proceeded up over the bridge and passed the second guard house at the foot of the bridge. *Nobody came, out! – we were in the clear*!

We stopped about 9:00 PM in a small village and entered a house right on the main street. We were led to a large room that could comfortably hold us all. They gave us a cold meal and a drink of Dutch gin. Soon someone started to sing and others joined in. The idea was to make enough noise so it would appear that we were celebrating. This was to throw off any observer as to just why we were there. There was a young girl about twenty three years of age in the group. Later, I found out that she had been the one that had arranged our escape and after the war I learned that she had been captured and shot by the Germans. At one point, she asked for part of my identification papers, the Ausweis, so that it might be used if somebody else came through that way. We were left to our singing and at about 11:30 PM we all fell asleep. We were awakened at 3:30 AM, mounted our bicycles and were on our way. Our next stop was at a stone factory on the Rhine River.

The factory manager led us to the power house and pulled a wooden cover off of an under-ground crib. We all went down a ladder into the dark dungeon and the cover was slid back over the top. There were others already in the crib. They were three Belgian young men who had deserted from a German labor camp. At dawn, we could see light filtering down through five holes in the crib top. It was enough so that we could barely make each other out. Dim as it was, it helped rid me of the creepy feeling I had during those earlier dark hours of being swallowed up in a dark, dank cave.

At about noon, the manager brought us another meal of bread and cold pork. Just after sundown, the lid was slid way back and we were told to climb out. We followed the factory manager up to his house and sat down to an absolutely unbelievable delicious dinner – beef roast, mashed potatoes, two vegetables, desert and coffee. It well made up for the long wait in the tomb.

At 11:30 PM, we left the cheery warmth of the manager's house and were led to the bank of the Rhine River. There in front of us in the water with its bow pulled up on the bank was a large steel boat. I was instructed to sit in the rear and steer with a large oar fitted in to an oarlock mounted on the stern that acted as a tiller. Joseph would sit up front and row and the seven others would lie in the bottom of the boat between us. We all moved to our assigned positions and the manager cast us off into the stream of the Rhine River. We were to cross the river and hug the left bank so that we would be sure to go down the Wahl River and not the continuation of the Rhine.

Our point of embarkation was just above the place where the Rhine River split into the Wahl and the Rhine. The southern branch, the Wahl, would carry us to freedom in the city of Nijmegen. The northern branch, which was a continuation of the Rhine, would carry us to Arnhem ("The Bridge Too Far") which was still held by the Germans. We had to be sure to cross far enough to avoid being carried down the Rhine. But, there was a problem — further up the Rhine, the Germans had blown up several dams to flood the areas there and deter the advance of the Allies. This excess water had advanced to the section of the river that we were in so that we could not find the river bank on the far side. We were being carried over farmer's fields, parts of roads, and sometimes the actual river bottom. The current was strong and all we could do was to keep the boat headed down stream and hope for the best.

Two things were in our favor — one, the moon was not shining and two, the Allies started a major offensive that night to push further into Germany. We would not easily be detected. We drifted with the current for several hours and then in the distance we could see a battery of lights directed over the surface of the water. We were shielded from those lights and would have to go around a sharp bend to the left before we would drift into them. We were not sure whether we should go out into the lights, wave our shirts and hope somebody would come out and get us, or whether we should pull up on shore and wait until morning to determine just where we were. We were not sure that we had actually gone down the Wahl. If we had continued down the Rhine then we would still be in German held territory. We decided to go to shore and wait.

We had been told that if we were able to get near Nijmegen, we should proceed with great caution since there was a good chance that the banks of the river would be mined. When the boat drove up on shore, those in front started to get out of the boat. Joseph grabbed the first one and held him back. By this time, I had moved to the front of the boat and Joseph took out his wallet and gave it to me. He told us to remain where we were until he came back. He then proceeded to move up a path that led to an abandoned stone factory and as he went, he frequently stomped the ground where he thought we would have to walk. He was willing to sacrifice himself to save us. Even now, I get a catch in my throat every time I recall his act of bravery.

When we were all up in the stone factory, we could make out the super-structure of a very large bridge in the distance. Was it the bridge in Arnhem or the bridge in Nijmegen? We had a strong feeling that we had missed the Wahl and had gone down the Rhine into German held territory. We were greatly despaired. There was no turning back. We would have to wait until dawn to find out.

As it got lighter, we could see vehicles through the light fog in the distance moving across a dike, but we could not identify them or the uniforms of the drivers. Finally, right within one hundred yards of us, we saw a motorcycle go by and then stop not far away. We went down to investigate and upon examining the motorcycle we saw that it was made in London, England. We yelled to the rider who was returning and one of the Dutch boys asked him in Dutch as to where we were and *he answered in English*! We were in Nijmegen – now held by the Canadians.

We were taken to a field artillery battery not four hundred yards from the stone factory. Canadian Intelligence Officers were called in to give us a preliminary interrogation. We had to prove that we were actually American pilots. They also questioned us as to just how we were able to get that close to the bridge. Joseph, the other Dutch boys, and the three

Belgians were taken to another camp and we did not see them again.

We turned over the maps and related to the interrogating officer our intentions to go out into the lights the previous night. He told us that those lights were shining across the water so that the 20mm and 40mm guns that were mounted on the shore could shoot anything that appeared in the water.

When the Germans retreated over the Wahl, they failed to destroy the bridge in Nijmegen. A heroic Dutchman raced out onto the bridge as the Germans departed and pulled all the fuses to the dynamite charges that had been set up to blow the bridge apart. Since then, the Germans had been sending mines attached to logs and frogmen down the river to still try to destroy the bridge. We were told that if we had gone into the lights, we would have been shot into bits because they felt that the Germans would try anything to accomplish their mission.

We were issued Canadian uniforms including toilet articles and then moved into a large hospital where there were no other patients. As I mentioned, the night we went down the Rhine, here was very heavy shelling by artillery as the Canadians started a push into Germany just East of Nijmegen. When we awoke in the morning, the yard was filled — mostly with Canadian soldiers who had had one or both of their feet blown off by shoe mines. There were also three or four German soldiers with them as well as an English bomber crew that had bailed out in that area.

We were treated very well by the Canadians and two days after our arrival, we were driven to Brussels where we stayed for three days. From there, we were flown to Paris for interrogation and a seven day visit. Then I was flown to London. Here I was interrogated by a young West Point Lieutenant who upon seeing me in a Canadian uniform remarked, "Thank God you're not another one of those God damn fly boys." I said, "Sorry Lieutenant, but I am an American P-51 Pilot." He stood up, pushed his chair back and slowly crawled under his desk. He then said, "Tell me when I can come out." It really was quite funny. He made out an envelope addressed to me in Milwaukee. He said that he had to keep the "deaf and dumb" documents to file with his report, but that they would then be forwarded to me. At that point I doubted that I would ever see them again. While in England, I decided to go to a well known Emblem Shop in an attempt to get an English "Catapillar Insignia" for my uniform. This is an award given by the British to any of their soldiers who have "walked out of enemy territory." While in this shop, I recognized a pilot from my brother Ken's Bomb Group and asked him to tell Ken that I was OK and back safe in London.

Later, I learned that he went back to camp, went to a movie, and saw Ken there. After he gave Ken the news, my brother yelled and hollered so much that they turned all the lights on and stopped the movie until everything calmed down.

From London, I went back to Wing Headquarters and lived like a king. I flew the General's brand new P51-D to visit my brother Ken and my own air base. Occasionally, I was asked to fly the piggy-back P51 (two seater) to take various officers to different Wing bases. I also was scheduled to visit several air bases and relate what had happened to me in an attempt to aid other pilots should they be shot down. Remembering just how much what Chuck Yeager told me had actually saved my life, I was more than willing to relate my experience to others.

Toward the end of March, I received orders to be returned to the States. We crossed on the Mauritania out of Glasgow and landed in Nova

Scotia. Shortly thereafter, I was given a thirty day leave and returned to Milwaukee.

After my leave, I was assigned to an Air Corps Pilots Pool in Selina, Alabama. Here's where I was finally instructed on how to bail out of an airplane and how to pull my chute open – just a little too late. I knew more than the instructor – I had had actual experience.

From here, I was assigned to Instrument Training School in Bryant, Texas. This was just what I needed. We learned how to fly instruments through thick cloud cover, which is something I had done on most every mission over in England. But, it passed the time.

After V-J day, I went to the Commandant's office at the Bryan Air Station and asked to be discharged. Upon looking up my record the Major in charge said, "No go, you signed up for the war plus six months unless, of course, you are an Escapee or an Evadee." At the time, I was standing at attention in front of his desk. He was irritated that I would ask, knowing how I had signed up in the first place. He immediately changed his attitude when I told him I was an Evadee! He suddenly became very understanding, asking me to sit down while he prepared the orders for my release from the Army.

So, within two weeks I was a civilian but still in the reserve. When I arrived home, there was the envelope containing my "Deaf and Dumb" identification papers which I now cherish very much.

I flew AT-6's out of O'Hare field in 1946, but gave it up when I discovered that flying once a month was not enough to keep up my proficiency. I have never flown since and I don't miss it. I have visited my friends in Holland many times and will continue to do so in the years to come. Most have passed away, but Miep is still alive and well and we enjoy each other's company just as we did during the War.

In 1985, a Rose Nursery was being constructed in the exact location where my P-51 went into the ground after I had bailed out. During several of my visits to Angeren, I had stood over that exact spot and had taken pictures of it. I received a phone call from Gijs who had come over to Idaho after the war. He told me that he had heard about the excavation that was necessary in order to erect the nursery and that they had recovered parts from my airplane. However, he stated that they would not let anybody have the parts. The Dutch Army was called in to retrieve the plane and the unexploded ammunition.

I pondered on what, to do and came upon the idea of writing a letter to the Queen of The Netherlands. I called the Milwaukee Public Library and was given the address, title, and the proper protocol in addressing the Queen. I wrote thanking her for the bravery of her people in risking their lives to save me and told her of my being desirous of obtaining parts from my plane.

Several weeks later, Gijs called me again. His first words were, "Howard, did you write the Queen?"

I said, "Yes. Why do you ask?"

He said, "Because they are shipping you several parts. The Queen sent one of her Aides, a Major, to the excavation and he ordered the parts to be released." A Mr. Heiting from Angeren generously had the parts packed and shipped by air directly to me.

I now have a twisted propeller blade, the propeller hub, two cylinders, a brake pedal, a motor valve, and other miscellaneous pieces.

When I last visited Angeren, we stopped to see the Rose Nursery and on the front of the building was a large painting of a P-51 with the 357th Fighter Group cowling insignia of red and yellow checkers.

The name of the nursery? What else but "The Mustang!"

In late summer of 1995, I received a call from my older brother, Carl, who told me that he had just received a package from Gijs. The next day, I went to visit him and picked up the package. Thinking it was a book of some sort, I did not open the package immediately, but waited until I got home.

There to my great surprise and amazement was a section of the wood post in which I had carved the dates of my stay in the shed. It seems that a Dutch farmer who knew Gijs cut out this section of the post and took it with him when he immigrated to Salt Lake City thinking that somebody might be interested in having it. However, the piece of wood lay in his basement for over fifty years. After he died, his daughter found it and arraigned to send it to Gijs since she remembered that he had had something to do with several downed pilots.

When I saw it, I was so thrilled that I cried. I couldn't believe what I was holding in my hands. It now decorates one of the shelves in our bookcase thanks to my dear friend, Gijs, and a very thoughtful lady who remembered what he had done during the War. Gijs and I stay in contact with each other and I correspond with Miep. Wout died several years ago as did Mr. Stevens and Mrs. Kok. I have lost contact with the Stevens children as well as the Kok children. It was fortunate that we were able to make several visits to Holland directly after the War and were able to see all of those who helped me.

I have written this story so that there is a record available should any of my grandchildren ever ask – "What did Grandpa do during the War?"

Afterword

by Mariah Montoya

After the war, Gys and Moebius maintained a close friendship over the phone, although they didn't see each other face to face until 1973, almost thirty years after Gys left the American pilot in his apple shed with a "Deaf and Dumb" paper.

Then, twenty-five years after immigrating to America, Gys and his wife hosted a party to celebrate their anniversary with both each other and America. Toward the middle of the party, in walked Howard Moebius from Wisconsin. Their wives had planned the reunion in secret. The two friends reunited and recalled old times, good and bad. Their connection was inseparable, unbreakable, still strong after all those years. And it remained so until the very end.

In 2006, Moebius called Gys at 3 o'clock in the morning and said, "Promise me our story will never be forgotten. The story must be told." At the time, he was on the floor, struggling to breathe or move. Gys promised his friend that he would do everything possible to get their story out there.

Howard Moebius passed away just hours later from a heart attack, and Gys took his promise to heart.

Gys wrote down three entire volumes of his lifetime, the first one concerning his life during the war. However, while Gys's memory is astonishing, he is constantly telling me, "But I am not a writer. And that's where you come in."

Needing someone to fix his volumes to be publishable, he asked the manager of The Cottages where he lives to find an author. The manager contacted the English teachers at my school, requesting a student willing to take on the project, and my English teacher asked me. I met Gys within a week, and read his war volume in a day. I don't think Gys realizes how powerful and impactful his words are! His descriptions and stories never ceased to amaze me, and while co-writing his story, I learned things I never, *ever* would have known otherwise. Sometimes History books don't press events into our minds as real or valuable until you realize that someone living and breathing actually went through them.

After the war, Gys was decorated by the Dutch, Canadian, British, and American governments for being resilient, brave, and a fighter. Shortly after, when he was twenty-nine years old, he met Zwaantje ten Berge (pronounced "Swan" in America). He married her on September 8, 1948. They are still married today, sitting across their room's table from each other every time I go to visit. I adore Swan. Whenever we part, she takes my hands in hers and just holds them for a while. So does Gys, always with a "Thank you, thank you, thank you, Mariah."

Before Gys married Swan, he had become fascinated with the idea of emigrating to America. He always idolized the Americans – remember the portrait of his uncle hanging up on his wall before the farm burned? He constantly thought about heading for a brighter future.

So in October of 1948, just a month after his marriage, he and his youngest brother Evert left for America on the ship *Erny Pyle*. The plan was for Gys to get a steady job so that he could support Swan before she herself joined him.

The leaving was hard. Gys's mother had died some months before. The last words his sick father said to Gys and his brother were: "Boys, I am very likely never to see you again. But whatever you do, always keep the honor to yourselves and always remain gentlemen, no matter what." Gys, indeed, never saw his father again. He passed away in 1972, before Gys ever made it back to Holland.

Gys did find work, though – eventually. His patriotism for America grew. When Swan finally reunited with him, she became homesick in the most devastating ways: nightmares, crying all night, longing for home to the point of getting physically sick. She must have had a trace of PTSD, too, for she had witnessed many atrocities in another part of Holland as well. During the war, as a girl, she had lived in Westerbork, and saw Jews arrive by the trainloads every day. Immediately after the war, she worked as a secretary in Westerbork's city hall, helping keep record of the long lists of people who would never return home.

War doesn't just hurt those it kills.

Gys and Swan moved from Utah, to California, and finally to Idaho, where they are still living today. They were blessed with three healthy children, Helen, Koop, and Henne Janice. After a lifetime of struggle, they are now in their nineties and living in a home. They are happy together, despite everything that has happened to them. Gys became an inventor. He invented many tools used by firefighters or rescue workers, including the Trucker's Friend, the Fireman's Ax, and the Ball Hammer. He and Swan are still hoping to return to their dairy farm when they are healthy enough again.

The biggest question Gys had throughout the war was "Why?" Why did so many people fall for Hitler's propaganda? Why would humans be so violent toward their own kind?

He thought that it all stemmed from hate. More specifically, the ill-fated Versailles peace agreement signed in late 1918. The severe amputations of Germany after World War I left the country crippling with economic consequences. Through all this, terrifying feelings of hate and revenge started smoldering fires. The suffering Germans were just waiting for someone to come along and turn their fire into an inferno.

This is when Hitler fell from the heavens. He had more than enough to complain about, and he was – however terribly, horribly, disgustingly – still a great leader. The book he wrote (or told somebody to write) in prison spelled out how to revive Germany from its suffering. But his rebuilding plan was one of destruction rather than *con*struction.

The result? When Hitler finally came to full power in 1933, the German people stood like one person behind him and his satanic ideals and plans.

Through hate, lust of revenge, and idealism, a monster was created.

And as for the Hitler Youth? I think Gys's own words are sufficient here. Reflecting upon the war, he says:

"The young children grew up in a hostile atmosphere after their bitter defeat. They were sired and reared by survivors of that war, but filled with vengeance and hate, not only caused by their defeat, but by the awful struggle to survive in bitterness and poverty. I can still remember Hitler crying out, 'The youth is our future, always!' This was true, but not while they were pumped up full of burning hate and revenge. Especially toward the Jewish people, whom Hitler blamed for Germany's failure and for monopolizing the business world. When he and his henchman laid down their Nazi foundation, they used the wrong ingredients. Period!"

"That's what the young soldiers were filled with when I watched them riding by in endless columns of tanks and motorized equipment. *Blitzkrieg* – lightning war, that is – was their motto. That new word was on everybody's lips and minds. In reality, it was nothing but barbaric murder in a highly organized method, and *that's* why it ultimately failed…"

If Gys were saying this to you right now, he would probably be staring in your direction, though unfocused, since he is now blind. All the same, something in his eyes would hold a determination and passion that would make you question the life you live: the everyday acts of going to school or work, the driving, the talking...Here in front of you is one of the last memory-holders of World War II, the war that seems like a dream or a fairy tale to most of us. Something that never affected us. Something in the past.

But the battle never ends. You must never forget to fight with goodness and kindness. This is what Gys is trying to relay. I believe this is also what Moebius was trying to say by writing down his own story. "You might just be one person," Gys has told me, "but the only way to mend the world is to start with yourself."

"While young minds nowadays are crammed full of useful knowledge and ideas, the real basics of right and wrong are sometimes neglected. Every day in our younger years, mental development grows. When life is fairly easy and smooth, one has less opportunity to prove him or herself."

"But sooner or later, trust me, character and true grit of one's worth is tested. That is when the real basics come to the foreground. Then you have to choose right from wrong. Don't forget that."

Appendix

This is a transcript of a letter from Gijs Jansen van Beek (Angeren)— the young man who first picked me up in the field where I had landed

February 1. 1945

Dear Howard,

Here is all good. and I know by you also from the letter to B. Stevens. I have read this. I was very happy but you know that I better self had had a letter from you. I think you have not received my first letter in June of this year.

After I was going away out of Angeren with the family Stevens but without you. I could not sleep that you remained alone behind there. And so I succeeded to get a Red Cross motorcar in order to haul a wounded brother from mine on the 2nd November.

I came in the shed but it was empty. Then I sought a note from you but I saw alone these letters in the boards from the shed.

OCT
M 16, 17
18, 19, 20
21, 22, 23,
24

From this I knew that you were away but were ok. That was a disappointment for me, but so it must be. Some days after that I heard that you had evacuated with the family Van Straaten.

I hope you receive this letter. After my examination in June 1946 I hope to visit America.
With kindest regards — your friend
//Gijs Jansen Van Beek//

Letter from Gys to Moebius

**HEADQUARTERS
UNITED STATES STRATEGIC AIR FORCES
IN EUROPE
Office of the Commanding General
APO 559**

General Orders)   10 October 1944
Number 999)

I.Under the provisions of Army Regulations 600-45, 22 September 1943,and pursuant to authority contained in letter 200.6, Headquarters Eighth Air force, dated 23 September 1944, Subject: "Awards and Decorations.

"The AIR MEDAL" is awarded to the following-named officer,for extraordinary achievement as set forth in citation.

HOWARD E. MOEBIUS, 0704711, First Lieutenant, Army Air Forces, United States Army. For extraordinary achievement while piloting a fighter type aircraft on a combat operation over enemy occupied territory, 18 September 1944. In a valiant attempt to defend his squadron from an attack by enemy fighters, Lieutenant Moebius courageously engaged a force of 12 ME-109's singlehandedly. His skillful maneuvers and daring aggressiveness enabled him to destroy one enemy aircraft. The bravery, disregard of personal safety, and superior airman ship displayed by Lieutenant Moebius on this occasion reflect the highest credit upon himself and the Army Air Forces.

BY COMMAND OF MAJOR GENERAL PARTRIDGE:

N. B. Harbold
Brigadier General, USA
Chief of Staff

OFFICIAL:/s/ John P. Thomas,
/t/ JOHN F. THOMAS
Major, Air Corps.

Decorations to Howard Moebius, from N. B. Horboid and E. P. Curtis

Gys and classmates, exact date unknown

Gys on a plow in 1942

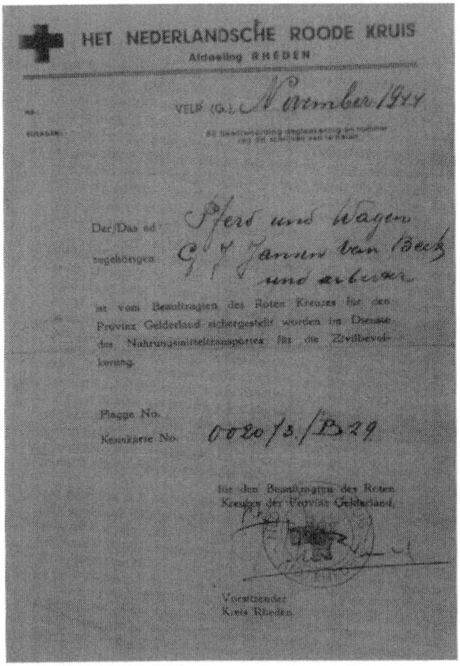

HET NEDERLANDSCHE ROODE KRUIS
Afdeeling RHEDEN

VELP (G.), November 1944

Der/Das ud Pferd und Wagen
zugehörigen G. J. Jansen van Beek
und arbeiter

ist vom Beauftragten des Roten Kreuzes für den Provinz Gelderland sichergestellt worden im Dienste des Nahrungsmitteltransportes für die Zivilbevölkerung.

Flagge No.
Kennkarte No. 0020/3./B29

für den Beauftragten des Roten Kreuzes der Provinz Gelderland,

Vorsitzender
Kreis Rheden.

Red Cross document

Gys's *Ausweis* from Lt. Themans

Lt. Themans and German companion

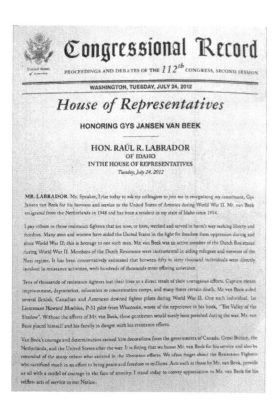

Congressional Record

PROCEEDINGS AND DEBATES OF THE 112th CONGRESS, SECOND SESSION

WASHINGTON, TUESDAY, JULY 24, 2012

House of Representatives

HONORING GYS JANSEN VAN BEEK

HON. RAÚL R. LABRADOR
OF IDAHO
IN THE HOUSE OF REPRESENTATIVES
Tuesday, July 24, 2012

MR. LABRADOR. Mr. Speaker, I rise today to ask my colleagues to join me in recognizing my constituent, Gys Jansen van Beek for his heroism and service to the United States of America during World War II. Mr. van Beek emigrated from the Netherlands in 1948 and has been a resident in my state of Idaho since 1954.

I pay tribute to those resistance fighters that are now, or have, worked and served in harm's way seeking liberty and freedom. Many men and women have aided the United States in the fight for freedom from oppression during and since World War II; this is homage to one such man. Mr. van Beek was an active member of the Dutch Resistance during World War II. Members of the Dutch Resistance were instrumental in aiding refugees and enemies of the Nazi regime. It has been conservatively estimated that between fifty to sixty thousand individuals were directly involved in resistance activities, with hundreds of thousands more offering assistance.

Tens of thousands of resistance fighters lost their lives as a direct result of their courageous efforts. Capture meant imprisonment, deportation, relocation to concentration camps, and many times certain death. Mr. van Beek aided several British, Canadian and American downed fighter pilots during World War II. One such individual, 1st Lieutenant Howard Moebius, P-51 pilot from Wisconsin, wrote of the experience in his book, "The Valley of the Shadow". Without the efforts of Mr. van Beek, these gentlemen would surely have perished during the war. Mr. van Beek placed himself and his family in danger with his resistance efforts.

Van Beek's courage and determination earned him decorations from the governments of Canada, Great Britain, the Netherlands, and the United States after the war. It is fitting that we honor Mr. van Beek for his service and also be reminded of the many others who assisted in the liberation efforts. We often forget about the Resistance Fighters who sacrificed much in an effort to bring peace and freedom to millions. Acts such as those by Mr. van Beek, provide us all with a model of courage in the face of atrocity. I stand today to convey appreciation to Mr. van Beek for his selfless acts of service to our Nation.

Congressional Record thanking Gys for his help to America during WWII, from Hon. Raúl R. Labrador

19340030R00144

Made in the USA
San Bernardino, CA
22 February 2015